THE FLAG OF THE FREE

Under the Stars and the Stripes,
  Protected in every way,
Live people of many types,
  Free to speak, to work, and to pray.

THE

AMERICAN

WAY

by

GERTRUDE VAN DUYN SOUTHWORTH

and

JOHN VAN DUYN SOUTHWORTH, M.A.

Master of History and Social Studies
Brunswick School, Greenwich, Connecticut

Co-authors of

America's Old World Background
The Thirteen American Colonies
Early Days in America
American History, Complete

IROQUOIS PUBLISHING COMPANY, INC.
SYRACUSE, NEW YORK

New York   Chicago   Atlanta   Dallas

Acknowledgments

Grateful acknowledgment is made to authors, authors' agents, and publishers for permission to reprint the following material:

Selections from a speech by Dr. Payson Smith; used by permission of The Antioch Press, Yellow Springs, Ohio. "Nancy Hanks," by Rosemary Benét; from *A Book of Americans*, published by Farrar & Rinehart, Inc. Copyright, 1933, by Rosemary and Stephen Vincent Benét. "God Bless America," by Irving Berlin; used by permission of Irving Berlin, Inc., New York. "The United States Not a Warlike Nation," from *The Rosary and Other Poems*, by Robert Cameron Rogers; used by permission of Dodd, Mead & Company, Inc. "Paul Revere's Ride" and "The Ship of State," by Henry Wadsworth Longfellow, and "Concord Hymn," by Ralph Waldo Emerson; used by permission of Houghton Mifflin Company, Boston. "The Blue and the Gray," by Francis Miles Finch; used by permission of Henry Holt and Company, Inc., New York. "The Warship of 1812"; used by permission of *The Philadelphia Record*. "The Flag Goes By," by Henry Holcomb Bennett; used by permission of *The Youth's Companion*, Detroit.

PREFACE

Today there are many influences at work throughout the world to discredit democracy, our American form of government. Hence, more than ever, it becomes necessary that the youth of our land, and all Americans, know well the story of our country, understand how our democracy has been built, and possess a true appreciation of the patriots whose great vision and sacrifice made possible many of the blessings we now enjoy.

To this end THE AMERICAN WAY goes back to the days of our Pilgrim fathers and follows through the principal events which have led to the development of our American way of life. The book presents the speeches with which patriotic Americans have fired the hearts of their listeners and kindled the spirit which has enabled our country to survive her great crises and to gain new strength with each survival. The speeches which these earnest patriots made will find an echo in the hearts of all true Americans. Included, also, are poems which ring with patriotic appeal.

The background of each crisis is given in an appropriate introduction, the introductions forming a consecutive chain linking together the events which have played so important a part in the evolution of our country.

The book ends with a summary of those blessings which our democracy confers on all people living within its borders, as well as the obligations which we all owe to the United States.

THE AUTHORS

iii

TABLE OF CONTENTS

PAGE

Preface iii

DEMOCRACY

The Growth of Democracy 1
Our First Democratic Document 7
The "Mayflower Compact" 7

THE STRUGGLE FOR INDEPENDENCE

The Thirteen Colonies Assert Their Rights . . 9
Patrick Henry Sounds the Call from Virginia 15
Give Me Liberty or Give Me Death.
. . . . *Patrick Henry* 17
Lexington and Concord 22
Paul Revere's Ride. *Henry W. Longfellow* . 24
Concord Hymn. *Ralph Waldo Emerson* . . 29
Thomas Paine—A World Patriot in the Cause
of Independence 30
Common Sense 30
The Crisis 31
Independence Marches On 33
The Declaration of Independence 33
The Glad Tidings Are Spread 41
Independence Bell. *Author Unknown* . . . 41
John Adams Speaks through Daniel Webster . 46
"Sink or Swim." *Daniel Webster* 47
The Stars and Stripes 53
The Flag Goes By. *Henry Holcomb Bennett* . 54

FRAMING THE GOVERNMENT FOR OUR NATION

The Drafting of Our Constitution 57
The Framework of Our Constitution . . . 58

PAGE

Adoption of the Constitution 61
   Franklin Urges the Adoption of the
      Constitution 61
Amendments to the Constitution 65

THE STRUGGLES OF THE NEW NATION

Washington and His "Farewell Address" . . . 66
Our Nation Not for Sale 71
National Unity Is Strengthened 73
   Hail, Columbia! *Joseph Hopkinson* 73
Thomas Jefferson, a True Democrat 77
   Quotations from Thomas Jefferson's First
      Inaugural Address 78
The United States Completes Her Independence 81
   The Freedom of the Seas, from a Report of the
      Committee on Foreign Relations, Novem-
      ber, 1811 82
Our Navy in the War of 1812 85
   The Warship of 1812. *Philadelphia Record* . 85
Our Most Popular National Anthem 88
   The Star-Spangled Banner. *Francis Scott Key* 89
The Monroe Doctrine 91
   The Americas for Americans.
     . . . . *President James Monroe* 93
The Greatest Speech of the Greatest American
   Orator 95
   Liberty and Union. *Daniel Webster* 97
Longfellow Describes the Republic 106
   The Ship of State. *Henry W. Longfellow* . . 106
The Nation Rejoices in Song 108
   America. *Reverend Samuel F. Smith* 108

PAGE

Public Education and Democracy 111
Horace Mann, Educator and Statesman.
. . . . *Dr. Payson Smith* 115

THE WAR BETWEEN THE STATES

The Question of Human Slavery 121
A House Divided against Itself.
. . . . *Abraham Lincoln* 122
Lincoln during the War between the States . . 123
Lincoln's Gettysburg Address 124
Lincoln Is Re-elected President 126
From Abraham Lincoln's Second Inaugural
Address 127
The Question of Slavery Is Settled 128
The Blue and the Gray. *Francis Miles Finch* 128
"You Wouldn't Know about My Son?" . . . 131
Nancy Hanks. *Rosemary Benét* 131
Liberty Enlightening the World 133

OUR COUNTRY THE FOE OF OPPRESSION

The Little War That Freed Cuba 137
President McKinley's War Message 138
Senator Lodge's Speech on War with Spain . 141
The United States Not a Warlike Nation.
. . . . *Robert Cameron Rogers* 145
Dewey's Flagship, the *Olympia* 150
The *Olympia* Speaks. *Author Unknown* . . 151

THE MODERN PERIOD

Why We Entered the First World War . . . 153
President Wilson's War Message 157

PAGE

President Wilson and the Peace with Germany 172
President Wilson's Veto Message 174
Women's Right to Vote 179
Democracy Is Again Threatened 185
The United States—The Good Neighbor . . . 187
The Need for Co-operation between the
Americas. *Cordell Hull* 189
President Roosevelt's Defiance of the Dictators 199
From President Roosevelt's Speech of December 29, 1940 199
The United States Enters the Second World War 210
President Roosevelt's War Message 211
President Roosevelt's Speech of December 9, 1941 214
At War with Germany and Italy 226
Our Declaration of War 226
Is Democracy Worth Fighting For? 227
Loyalty to Flag and Country 229
The Pledge of Allegiance 229
The American's Creed. *William Tyler Page* 229
True Patriotism. *Sir Walter Scott* 230
God Bless America. *Irving Berlin* 231
The Old Flag Forever. *Frank L. Stanton* . 231

APPENDIX

The Constitution of the United States 1
Amendments to the Constitution 15
Quotations from Washington's "Farewell Address" 24

DEMOCRATIC GOVERNMENT BEGINS IN AMERICA

In taking his oath of office, Washington, our first President, pledged to "preserve, protect, and defend the Constitution of the United States," which grants freedom of speech, freedom of religion, and self-government to all citizens.

DEMOCRACY

THE GROWTH OF DEMOCRACY

What is this "Democracy" we hear so much about today? Abraham Lincoln expressed it simply when he said it is "government of the people, by the people, for the people."

We Americans are likely to think of democracy as the natural form of government for all men. We are used to freedom of speech and to living as we like, subject only to laws of our own making. We do not stop to realize that few nations enjoy these privileges. In the past, most of mankind was held down and oppressed by kings and nobles. This small ruling class felt that those they governed must be kept so weak and ignorant that they would not have the strength or wisdom to rise against their oppressors.

Then, a little more than three hundred years ago, men from Europe began to cross the Atlantic Ocean and settle in North America. These people came from many lands, but most of them came with a common purpose—the finding of freedom. In the wilderness of the New World they made homes for themselves, and in these humble homes was born the dream of an America free from oppression.

This American Dream has not always remained the same. It has changed and developed, but always in

1

the same direction—toward a more complete freedom. At first the Dream was of a home where men would be free to think for themselves and to worship God as they saw fit. Later came the desire for complete independence. This independence was finally won by force of arms, and a new nation without kings and without nobles arose. Still the Dream developed. Gradually the right to take an active part in their government was extended to people who had never enjoyed that privilege before—to men of little or no property, to citizens of all races, and at last to women. Democracy in America came to mean government by *all* the people—not by just a chosen few.

As the seeds of democracy grew and flourished in America, our people saw with joy that the dream of freedom from oppression was spreading to other lands. The people of France arose in 1789, overthrew their king and their nobles, and established a republic of their own. The Spanish colonies of the New World, following the example of the United States, broke away from their mother country and set up independent governments. Other European countries, influenced by the spread of democracy, granted their people increasing rights. England, step by step, reduced the power of her king and her nobles until she became as democratic in many respects as our own country. By the year 1920 many of the world's countries were democracies, and the movement for man's freedom was sweeping the world like an irresistible tide.

Of course, this progress was not always peacefully attained. There were wars and revolutions, suffering and bloodshed. But the goal—human freedom—seemed well worth the price.

Then suddenly the tide was checked. It began to look as though man might face a bitter awakening from the sweet dream of freedom. Trouble began in Europe, where there was much turmoil as a result of the World War of 1914-1918. In the democratic kingdom of Italy, Benito Mussolini seized the reins of government and became dictator. A few years later Adolf Hitler came to power in Germany. The people of these countries no longer had a voice in their governments; everything depended upon the will of the dictators; freedom was gone. People who dared to criticize the government were imprisoned, punished, and sometimes even put to death. While the free peoples of the world looked on, only half realizing the importance of the catastrophe that was taking place, Mussolini and Hitler made an agreement to work together. Germany and Italy became known as the Axis powers.

The free nations of the world, still not realizing the danger which threatened them, were shocked when they saw Japan, a nation whose people enjoyed no freedom, invade the Chinese republic. Yet they did nothing about it. They saw Italy swallow up the countries of Ethiopia and Albania, and still they did nothing. They saw Germany take Austria and a part of Lithuania and threaten Czechoslovakia. Here the statesmen of France and Great Britain tried to stop these conquests by consenting to German control of a part of Czechoslovakia if Germany would promise to leave the rest of the country independent. The promise was made, but it meant nothing. Germany soon took over all of Czechoslovakia except a small section which went to Hungary. Germany then attacked Poland. Realizing at last that the freedom of all Europe was in danger, France and Great Britain went to war with Germany in a frantic attempt to stop the conquest of free peoples.

But the tide of conquest swept on. Almost at once Russia, another dictator-ruled country, entered the picture. She helped Germany defeat Poland, and she received, in return, a part of that stricken country. Russia also attacked Finland and won a part of it. Later, she annexed the free countries of Estonia, Latvia, and Lithuania. German armies swept through the Netherlands, Belgium, Denmark, Norway, and Luxembourg, adding these independent countries to those under the German dictator. Then Italy entered the war against Great Britain and France. France collapsed under the powerful attack of Germany and was forced to surrender. The success of the Axis powers attracted a new member, Japan. Hungary, encouraged by Germany, seized a part of Rumania; the rest of Rumania accepted German control without resistance. Bulgaria, invaded by German troops, decided that submission to Germany was the better course for her to take.

While Germany was engaged in making Axis partners of Hungary, Rumania, and Bulgaria, Italy attacked Greece. The Greeks fought so valiantly that Italy was forced to call upon Germany for help. Yugoslavia, through which German troops had to pass on their way to Greece, resisted fiercely, but to no avail. German might again proved too great, and Greece was forced to yield.

After the conquest of Greece the world wondered where Germany would strike next. But the wonder changed to surprise when German troops invaded Russia. Only two years before, Germany and Russia had signed a treaty in which each pledged not to go to war with the other for a period of ten years. But Russia stood in Hitler's way, and Hitler decided that Russia should bow to the German might.

Surprising as was Germany's attack on Russia, an event still more startling was to shock the world. On the pretext of securing friendly relations with our country, Japan sent a special envoy to discuss peace terms with President Roosevelt. While the talks were still going on, Japan without warning attacked the United States possession of Hawaii in the Pacific. She then declared war on the United States and Great Britain and launched attacks against their possessions in the Far East. Shocked and angered at the Japanese treachery, President Roosevelt called an urgent session of Congress, and our country at once declared war on Japan and took up arms in defense of democracy.

THE SIGNING OF THE "MAYFLOWER COMPACT"

In the little cabin of the *Mayflower* the seeds of American democracy were sown when the Pilgrims signed a compact to work together for the common good.

OUR FIRST DEMOCRATIC DOCUMENT

On the eleventh day of November, 1620, the little ship *Mayflower* dropped anchor at the tip of Cape Cod in the bay which is now the harbor of Provincetown, Massachusetts. On board were about one hundred men and women who had fled from England to escape the tyranny of King James I. Rather than submit to the king and surrender the rights to which they believed all men were entitled, these brave people had risked the dangers of a voyage across the ocean in a small and overcrowded ship and were now preparing to face the even greater hardships of life in an unknown wilderness.

Knowing well the dangers that faced them, and realizing the necessity of working together for the common good, these Pilgrims gathered in the cabin of their ship and drew up an agreement which has become known as the "Mayflower Compact."

The "Mayflower Compact" was not a constitution, for it contained no plan for a detailed government. It was merely an agreement to work together for the good of all. It was, however, the first document ever to contain the principles of government "by the people, for the people." Thus it is to us a priceless heritage, rightfully called "the germ of popular government in America."

THE MAYFLOWER COMPACT

In ye name of God, Amen. We whose names are underwritten, the loyall subjects of our dread soveraigne Lord, King James, by ye Grace of God of Great Britaine, France & Ireland King, Defender of ye Faith, etc. Haveing undertaken, for ye Glorie of God, and advancemente of ye Christian Faith and Honour of our King and countrie, a Voyage to plant ye first Colonie in ye Northerne part of Virginia, doe by these presents solemnly and mutually in ye Presence of God, and of another, Covenant & Combine our selves togeather into a Civill body Politick, for our better Ordering & Preservation & Furtherance of ye ends aforesaid; and by Vertue hereof to enact, constitute, and frame such just & equall lawes, ordinances, Acts, Constitutions & Offices, from Time to Time, as shall be thought most meete & convenient for ye generall good of ye Colonie, unto which we promise all due submission and obedience.

THE STRUGGLE FOR INDEPENDENCE

THE THIRTEEN COLONIES ASSERT THEIR RIGHTS

Even before the Pilgrims and Puritans came from England and settled on the bluff New England shores, other Englishmen had settled in Virginia. Dutch traders, too, had come from Holland and formed the colony of New Netherland.

Some years after the Puritans settled in Massachusetts, the English colonies of Maryland and Pennsylvania were founded along America's eastern coast. Colonists also came from Sweden and settled along Delaware Bay, but soon a Dutch army conquered the Swedish colony and made it part of New Netherland. When, in 1664, New Netherland was surrendered to the English, the land settled by the Swedes and the Dutch became the English colonies of New York, New Jersey, and Delaware.

Gradually settlers from the early colonies branched out and formed new colonies. Though the Puritans of Massachusetts had come to America in search of religious freedom, the laws by which they governed their colony were very strict. No one could worship as he liked in Massachusetts or do much of anything else according to his own ideas. Roger Williams, a young Puritan minister, felt this was wrong and said

9

THOMAS HOOKER AND HIS FOLLOWERS

Thomas Hooker, a Puritan minister, and his followers left the Massachusetts colony to seek a place where they could worship as they pleased. Traveling on foot, they reached the Connecticut Valley and there founded the town of Hartford.

so in his sermons. When the Puritan leaders threatened to send him back to England, he fled from the colony and made his way to the shores of Narragansett Bay. There, with a few friends who had joined him, he started the settlement of Providence. Others who agreed with Williams' ideas followed, and before long the colony of Rhode Island was established. In Rhode Island every man was allowed to vote, no matter what his religion was, and each could worship as he saw fit, for were not these the blessings for which they had come to America?

Other discontented colonists left Massachusetts and helped found the colonies of New Hampshire and Connecticut. The Connecticut colonists drew up the first written constitution in North America.

The Carolinas were founded by English settlers from Virginia and England.

When the southern colony of Georgia was founded by the English General Oglethorpe in 1733, it was the thirteenth English colony on America's Atlantic coast. English ownership of the colonies did not prevent people from other countries settling in them. From most of the countries of Europe men came to the American colonies. America to many of them was a haven of refuge, a land of opportunity, where every man hoped his dream of freedom would come true.

In the year that Georgia was founded, there occurred in the colony of New York an event which was to have far-reaching results. John Peter Zenger, editor and printer of the *New York Weekly Journal*, believed in printing the truth even though it might not please Governor Cosby. When some articles of Zenger's did displease the governor, he had Zenger thrown into prison. Did this mean that no printer could print the truth if it did not suit a governor to have it printed? The story of Zenger's arrest was told in Philadelphia where lived an able lawyer named Andrew Hamilton. Hamilton offered to go to New York and help Zenger, and so well did he plead the case that Zenger was acquitted. Freedom of the press thus was assured in the colonies and later it was written into the Constitution of the United States.

At first there were several different kinds of government in the colonies. Some colonies were governed by the owners to whom the English king had granted the land. Others had been founded by colonizing companies and were governed by these companies. Still others were governed by the colonists themselves.

In time the king of England took full possession of the colonies and gave them the same general type of government. Each colony had an Assembly made up of members who were chosen by the people to represent them. Each had a governor who represented the king of England. The governor and the Assembly worked together to make the laws for their colony. Because the governor could veto, or forbid, any law which the Assembly passed, he had more power than the Assembly.

Naturally, when the governor and the Assembly disagreed, the people sided with the Assembly, and gradually the confidence in such representative government grew. Moreover, for many years, the English king was too busy with affairs at home to bother much about his colonies in America, and the colonies grew accustomed to making their own decisions and to laying their own taxes.

When George III came to the throne of England in 1760, England's attitude toward her thirteen American colonies changed. King George, like other European monarchs, believed that colonies existed entirely for the benefit of the mother country. So he forbade the colonies to manufacture articles which competed with goods that were made in England, and required them to trade solely with the mother country. Taxes were also placed on various products that had to be imported. The colonists were far from pleased with King George's acts, and goods were smuggled into the colonies to avoid payment of the taxes.

To cut down this smuggling, the English government issued search warrants, called Writs of Assistance. Any officer who had a Writ of Assistance could enter any house or shop and search it from top to bottom without even saying for what he was searching.

The colonists felt that England had no right to issue the writs. James Otis made a stirring speech before the Massachusetts Assembly, opposing them. But still the searches continued.

Then came the Stamp Act, a law which said that a government stamp must be placed on all newspapers, pamphlets, wills, mortgages, and other legal and public papers. So bitterly did the colonists oppose the Stamp Act, and so determined were they not to accept the stamps, that England finally repealed the Act. Soon, however, the Townshend Acts were passed, placing a duty on window glass, paper, paint, and tea. Again the colonists refused to buy the goods and pay the duties. At last England repealed the tax on all but tea. Still the colonists refused to pay the tax on even this one article, and when three vessels loaded with tea reached Boston, the tea was dumped into the sea.

Furious now, King George and Parliament passed the "Intolerable Acts" as the colonists called them. These acts closed the port of Boston to all trade until the tea should be paid for, and took away privileges of self-government which the Massachusetts colonists prized highly. Moreover, the acts gave England the right to quarter English soldiers in the homes of the colonists. Already an English army of 10,000 soldiers had been sent to America, and the colonists were to bear the expense of supporting these troops.

A storm of indignation swept the colonies, and a meeting of colonial representatives was called to be held in Philadelphia in September, 1774. This First Continental Congress drew up a Declaration of Rights and Grievances which asked the king to repeal his unjust laws and demanded that the colonies be given the right to levy their own taxes. This appeal to England's king was ignored, and a general spirit of resentment united the colonies in a common cause.

PATRICK HENRY SOUNDS THE CALL FROM VIRGINIA

In Virginia the first great American champion of liberty made himself heard. It was in the city of Richmond, and Patrick Henry was speaking to the Virginia Assembly. The colonists had stood all the oppression they could from England's king, and the Assembly faced the serious question: What course shall we now follow?

Some of the members still hoped that England could be induced to repeal her unjust laws, and they wanted the door between them and the mother country left open so that if things changed for the better they might still be counted good Englishmen. But Patrick Henry thought differently. He believed that the colonies should no longer submit to British tyranny. They should go bravely out and slam the door behind them, he insisted, and he made a motion that Virginia raise an army of her own and put herself "in a posture of defense."

This was going too far for the conservative members. They were not ready for such extreme measures. They needed to be aroused, to be led to see that love of liberty must come ahead of love of England. So it remained for Patrick Henry to sound the call, and springing to his feet he made a speech that thrilled and swayed his hearers.

One who was there says, "Henry rose with an unearthly fire burning in his eyes. The tendons of his neck stood out white and rigid like whipcords. His voice rose louder and louder, until the walls of the building and all within them seemed to shake and rock. Finally his pale

Brown Brothers, N. Y.

PATRICK HENRY IN THE VIRGINIA ASSEMBLY

Urging that the American colonies throw off the tyrannical yoke of England, by means of war, if necessary, Patrick Henry ended with the cry, "I know not what course others may take; but as for me, give me liberty or give me death!"

face and glaring eye became terrible to look upon. His last exclamation, 'Give me liberty or give me death!' was like the shout of a leader which turns the rout of battle."

When Patrick Henry finished, the resolution which he had proposed was carried unanimously.

GIVE ME LIBERTY OR GIVE ME DEATH

Delivered by PATRICK HENRY at Richmond, in the Virginia Assembly, on a Resolution to Put the Commonwealth in a State of Defense, March 23, 1775.

MR. PRESIDENT:

No man thinks more highly than I do of the patriotism, as well as abilities, of the very worthy gentlemen who have just addressed the house. But different men often see the same subject in different lights; and, therefore, I hope it will not be thought disrespectful to those gentlemen, if, entertaining as I do opinions of a character very opposite to theirs, I shall speak forth my sentiments freely and without reserve. This is no time for ceremony. The question before the house is one of awful moment to this country. For my own part, I consider it as nothing less than a question of freedom or slavery; and in proportion to the magnitude of the subject ought to be the freedom of the debate. It is only in this way that we can hope to arrive at truth and fulfill the great responsibility which we hold to God and our country.

Should I keep back my opinions at such a time, through fear of giving offense, I should consider myself as guilty of treason towards my country, and of an act of disloyalty toward the Majesty of Heaven, which I revere above all earthly kings.

Mr. President, it is natural to man to indulge in the illusions of hope. We are apt to shut our eyes against a painful truth, and listen to the song of that siren, till she transforms us into beasts. Is this the part of wise men, engaged in a great and arduous struggle for liberty? Are we disposed to be of the number of those, who, having eyes, see not, and having ears, hear not, the things which so nearly concern their temporal salvation? For my part, whatever anguish of spirit it may cost, I am willing to know the whole truth; to know the worst, and to provide for it.

I have but one lamp by which my feet are guided, and that is the lamp of experience. I know of no way of judging of the future but by the past. And judging by the past, I wish to know what there has been in the conduct of the British ministry for the last ten years to justify those hopes with which gentlemen have been pleased to solace themselves and the house. Is it that insidious smile with which our petition has been lately received? Trust it not, sir; it will prove a snare to your feet.

Suffer not yourselves to be betrayed with a kiss. Ask yourselves how this gracious reception of our petition comports with those warlike preparations which cover our waters and darken our land. Are fleets and armies necessary to a work of love and reconciliation? Have we shown ourselves so unwilling to be reconciled, that force must be called in to win back our love? Let us not deceive ourselves, sir.

These are the implements of war and subjugation; the last arguments to which kings resort.

I ask gentlemen, sir, What means this martial array, if its purpose be not to force us to submission? Can gentlemen assign any other possible motive for it? Has Great Britain any enemy, in this quarter of the world, to call for all this accumulation of navies and armies? No, sir, she has none. They are meant for us: they can be meant for no other. They are sent over to bind and rivet upon us those chains which the British ministry have been so long forging.

And what have we to oppose to them? Shall we try argument? Sir, we have been trying that for the last ten years. Have we anything new to offer upon the subject? Nothing. We have held the subject up in every light of which it is capable; but it has been all in vain. Shall we resort to entreaty and humble supplication? What terms shall we find, which have not been already exhausted?

Let us not, I beseech you, sir, deceive ourselves longer. Sir, we have done everything that could be done, to avert the storm which is now coming on. We have petitioned; we have remonstrated; we have supplicated; we have prostrated ourselves before the throne, and have implored its interposition to arrest the tyrannical hands of the ministry and Parliament.

Our petitions have been slighted; our remonstrances have produced additional violence and insult; our supplications have been disregarded; and we have been spurned, with contempt, from the foot of the throne! In vain, after these things, may we indulge the fond hope of peace and reconciliation. There is no longer any room for hope.

If we wish to be free—if we mean to preserve inviolate those inestimable privileges for which we have been so long contending—if we mean not basely to abandon the noble struggle in which we have been so long engaged, and which we have pledged ourselves never to abandon until the glorious object of our contest shall be obtained—we must fight! I repeat it, sir, we must fight! An appeal to arms and to the God of Hosts is all that is left us!

They tell us, sir, that we are weak; unable to cope with so formidable an adversary. But when shall we be stronger? Will it be the next week, or the next year? Will it be when we are totally disarmed, and when a British guard shall be stationed in every house? Shall we gather strength by irresolution and inaction? Shall we acquire the means of effectual resistance by lying supinely on our backs and hugging the delusive phantom of hope, until our enemies shall have bound us hand and foot?

Sir, we are not weak, if we make a proper use of those means which the God of nature hath placed in our power. Three millions of people, armed in the holy cause of liberty, and in such a country as that which we possess, are invincible by any force which our enemy can send against us.

Besides, sir, we shall not fight our battles alone. There is a just God who presides over the destinies of nations, and who will raise up friends to fight our battles for us. The battle, sir, is not to the strong alone; it is to the vigilant, the active, the brave.

Besides, sir, we have no election. If we were base enough to desire it, it is now too late to retire from the contest. There is no retreat but in submission and slavery! Our chains are forged! Their clanking may be heard on the plains of Boston! The war is inevitable—and let it come! I repeat it, sir, let it come.

It is in vain, sir, to extenuate the matter. Gentlemen may cry, Peace, Peace—but there is no peace. The war is actually begun! The next gale that sweeps from the north will bring to our ears the clash of resounding arms! Our brethren are already in the field! Why stand we here idle? What is it that gentlemen wish? What would they have? Is life so dear, or peace so sweet, as to be purchased at the price of chains and slavery? Forbid it, Almighty God! I know not what course others may take; but as for me, give me liberty or give me death!

LEXINGTON AND CONCORD

Oppressed by the action of England's king, Massachusetts, like Virginia, decided to raise an army of her own. "Minutemen" her soldiers were called, because they promised to be ready to serve at a minute's notice. Their arms and ammunition were stored in Concord.

In Boston were the British troops under General Gage, sent to govern Massachusetts as punishment for what the king called rebellious conduct.

General Gage learned where the colonial arms were stored and planned to seize them. On the way to Concord his men were to capture John Hancock and Samuel Adams, colonial leaders staying in the town of Lexington.

The expedition was to be a secret one, moving under cover of the night. But in some mysterious way Paul Revere of Boston got wind of Gage's plan. Across the Mystic River he waited for a comrade to signal him, from the steeple of the Old North Church, news of the British advance.

No sooner had the lanterns flashed the signal than he sprang to his saddle, and dashing through the country toward Lexington and Concord, he roused all he passed with the cry, "To arms! To arms! The regulars are coming!"

No second warning was needed. While Hancock and Adams slipped quietly away from Lexington, the minutemen made ready for battle. When the English reached the town early in the morning, there on the village green they found a small but determined group of armed men ready to fight. With such uneven forces, the battle of

Brown Brothers, N. Y.

PAUL REVERE ROUSES THE MINUTEMEN

Warned that the British were on their way to Lexington and Concord, Paul Revere rode through the night rousing the colonists. "To arms! To arms!" he cried. "The regulars are coming."

Lexington was very short. The minutemen were driven off, and the English marched on to Concord.

Near the northern end of Concord was a wooden bridge. Here the English were met by a second band of minutemen who barred their way. The English opened fire, but, instead of retreating, the minutemen returned the fire and kept it up until the English were forced to fall back. Then, running through the woods and fields that bordered the road, the minutemen shot down red-coat after redcoat. Soon the English retreat became a rout as they fled back toward Boston.

PAUL REVERE'S RIDE

Henry Wadsworth Longfellow

Listen, my children, and you shall hear
Of the midnight ride of Paul Revere,
On the eighteenth of April, in Seventy-five;
Hardly a man is now alive
Who remembers that famous day and year.

He said to his friend: "If the British march
By land or sea from the town tonight,
Hang a lantern aloft in the belfry arch
Of the North Church tower as a signal light,—
One, if by land, and two, if by sea;
And I on the opposite shore will be,
Ready to ride and spread the alarm
Through every Middlesex village and farm,
For the country folk to be up and to arm."

Then he said "Good-night," and with muffled oar
Silently rowed to the Charlestown shore,
Just as the moon rose over the bay,
Where swinging wide at her moorings lay
The *Somerset*, British man-of-war;
A phantom ship, with each mast and spar
Across the moon like a prison bar,
And a huge black hulk, that was magnified
By its own reflection in the tide.

Meanwhile his friend, through alley and street,
Wanders and watches with eager ears,
Till in the silence around him he hears
The muster of men at the barrack-door,
The sound of arms, and the tramp of feet,
And the measured tread of the grenadiers
Marching down to their boats on the shore.

Then he climbed the tower of the Old North Church,
By the wooden stairs, with stealthy tread,
To the belfry-chamber overhead,
And startled the pigeons from their perch
On the sombre rafters, that round him made
Masses and moving shapes of shade,—
By the trembling ladder, steep and tall,
To the highest window in the wall,
Where he paused to listen and look down
A moment on the roofs of the town,
And the moonlight flowing over all.

Beneath, in the churchyard lay the dead
In their night-encampment on the hill,
Wrapped in silence so deep and still
That he could hear, like a sentinel's tread,
The watchful night-wind, as it went
Creeping along from tent to tent,
And seeming to whisper, "All is well!"
A moment only he feels the spell
Of the place and the hour, and the secret dread
Of the lonely belfry and the dead;

For suddenly all his thoughts are bent
On a shadowy something far away,
Where the river widens to meet the bay,—
A line of black that bends and floats
On the rising tide like a bridge of boats.

Meanwhile, impatient to mount and ride,
Booted and spurred, with a heavy stride
On the opposite shore walked Paul Revere.
Now he patted his horse's side,
Now gazed at the landscape far and near,
Then, impetuous, stamped the earth,
And turned and tightened his saddle-girth;
But mostly he watched with eager search
The belfry-tower of the Old North Church,
As it rose above the graves on the hill,
Lonely and spectral and sombre and still.
And lo! as he looks, on the belfry's height
A glimmer and then a gleam of light!
He springs to the saddle, the bridle he turns,
But lingers and gazes, till full on his sight
A second lamp in the belfry burns.

A hurry of hoofs in a village street,
A shape in the moonlight, a bulk in the dark,
And beneath, from the pebbles, in passing, a spark
Struck out by a steed flying fearless and fleet;
That was all! And yet, through the gloom and the
    light
The fate of a nation was riding that night;

And the spark struck out by that steed in his flight
Kindled the land into flame with its heat.

He has left the village and mounted the steep,
And beneath him, tranquil and broad and deep,
Is the Mystic, meeting the ocean tides;
And under the alders that skirt its edge,
Now soft on the sand, now loud on the ledge,
Is heard the tramp of his steed as he rides.
It was twelve by the village clock
When he crossed the bridge into Medford town.
He heard the crowing of the cock,
And the barking of the farmer's dog,
And felt the damp of the river's fog,
That rises after the sun goes down.

It was one by the village clock
When he galloped into Lexington.
He saw the gilded weathercock
Swim in the moonlight as he passed,
And the meetinghouse windows, blank and bare,
Gaze at him with a spectral glare,
As if they already stood aghast
At the bloody work they would look upon.

It was two by the village clock
When he came to the bridge in Concord town,
He heard the bleating of the flock,
And the twitter of birds among the trees,

And felt the breath of the morning breeze
Blowing over the meadows brown.
And one was safe and asleep in his bed
Who at the bridge would be first to fall,
Who that day would be lying dead,
Pierced by a British musket-ball.

You know the rest. In the books you have read
How the British regulars fired and fled,—
How the farmers gave them ball for ball,
From behind each fence and farmyard wall,
Chasing the redcoats down the lane,
Then crossing the fields to emerge again
Under the trees at the turn of the road,
And only pausing to fire and load.

So through the night rode Paul Revere;—
And so through the night went his cry of alarm
To every Middlesex village and farm,—
A cry of defiance, and not of fear,
A voice in the darkness, a knock at the door,
And a word that shall echo forevermore!
For, borne on the night-wind of the past,
Through all our history to the last,
In the hour of darkness, and peril, and need,
The people will waken and listen to hear
The hurrying hoof-beats of that steed,
And the midnight message of Paul Revere.

CONCORD HYMN

Ralph Waldo Emerson

The "Concord Hymn" was written to be sung at the unveiling of the Concord Monument, the statue of a minuteman, April 19, 1836.

By the rude bridge that arched the flood,
    Their flag to April's breeze unfurled,
Here once the embattled farmers stood,
    And fired the shot heard round the world.

The foe long since in silence slept;
    Alike the conqueror silent sleeps;
And Time the ruined bridge has swept
    Down the dark stream which seaward creeps.

On this green bank, by this soft stream,
    We set today a votive stone;
That memory may their deed redeem,
    When, like our sires, our sons are gone.

Spirit, that made those heroes dare
    To die and leave their children free,
Bid Time and Nature gently spare
    The shaft we raise to them and Thee.

THOMAS PAINE—A WORLD PATRIOT IN THE CAUSE OF INDEPENDENCE

Thomas Paine was born in England in 1737, but it would not be accurate to speak of him as an Englishman. In one sense he had no country, for he went wherever there was oppression or injustice and used his brain and his pen to help the people. During our Revolution, Thomas Paine was an outstanding American, and not long afterward he was just as good a Frenchman. Perhaps it would be best to call him "a citizen of the world."

Paine became acquainted with Benjamin Franklin on one of Franklin's visits to England on behalf of the colonies, and it was as a result of this meeting that he moved to America, in 1774. He settled in Pennsylvania.

COMMON SENSE

Early in the American Revolution, Paine was amazed to see the colonists fighting against the king's armies and yet insisting that they were loyal subjects of King George III of England. Such inconsistency seemed ridiculous to Thomas Paine, so he wrote a powerful pamphlet urging Americans to wake up and to realize that the real issue of the war was not gaining the "rights of Englishmen," whatever they might be, but gaining outright independence from the English government. This pamphlet, called *Common Sense*, was widely read; it was one of the important factors which led to the writing of the Declaration of Independence.

A Selection from *COMMON SENSE*

by Thomas Paine

The sun never shone on a cause of greater worth. 'Tis not the affair of a city, a county, a province, or a kingdom, but of a Continent—of at least one-eighth part of the habitable globe. 'Tis not the concern of a day, a year, or an age; posterity are virtually involved in the contest, and will be more or less affected even to the end of time, by the proceedings now.

THE CRISIS

In the dreadful winter of 1776, when George Washington's armies were shivering in their miserable little camp at Valley Forge, Paine once more took up his pen. His series of pamphlets, called *The Crisis*, which now appeared, urged the people of America to stand back of their army and their General in the hour of darkest need. It helped to revive hope when it was at a very low ebb; it did much to enable Washington to carry on the war and win our country's independence. We of America are much indebted to Thomas Paine, freedom-loving citizen of the world.

A Selection from *THE CRISIS*

by Thomas Paine

These are the times that try men's souls. The summer soldier and the sunshine patriot will, in this crisis, shrink from the service of his country; but he that stands it NOW deserves the love and thanks of man and woman. Tyranny is not easily conquered; yet we have this consolation with us, that the harder the conflict, the more glorious the triumph. What we obtain too cheap, we esteem too lightly: 'tis dearness only that gives everything its value.

Heaven knows how to put a proper price upon its goods; and it would be strange indeed if so celestial an article as FREEDOM should not be highly rated.

INDEPENDENCE MARCHES ON

When at last the American colonists saw that the time had come to break with the mother country, they appointed a committee to draw up a declaration of independence.

John Adams, Benjamin Franklin, Roger Sherman, Robert R. Livingston, and Thomas Jefferson were chosen for this work, but it was Thomas Jefferson who put into words the convictions and beliefs of the whole committee.

The declaration was submitted to the Continental Congress which met in Independence Hall, Philadelphia; and after much discussion the members, on July 4, 1776, voted for its adoption.

THE DECLARATION OF INDEPENDENCE

ADOPTED BY THE CONTINENTAL CONGRESS
July 4, 1776

THE UNANIMOUS DECLARATION OF THE THIRTEEN UNITED STATES OF AMERICA

When, in the course of human events, it becomes necessary for one people to dissolve the political bands which have connected them with another, and to assume among the powers of the earth the separate and equal station to which the laws of nature and of nature's God entitle them, a decent respect to the

Brown Brothers, N. Y.

DRAFTING THE DECLARATION OF INDEPENDENCE

The five men appointed to draw up the Declaration of Independence which declared the American colonies free from England. From right to left: Benjamin Franklin, Thomas Jefferson, John Adams, Roger Sherman, Robert Livingston.

opinions of mankind requires that they should declare the causes which impel them to the separation.

We hold these truths to be self-evident: That all men are created equal; that they are endowed by their Creator with certain unalienable rights; that among these are life, liberty, and the pursuit of happiness; that, to secure these rights, governments are instituted among men, deriving their just powers from the consent of the governed; that, whenever any form of government becomes destructive of these ends, it is the right of the people to alter or to abolish it, and to institute a new government, laying its foundation on such principles, and organizing its powers in such form, as to them shall seem most likely to effect their safety and happiness. Prudence, indeed, will dictate that governments long established should not be changed for light and transient causes; and, accordingly, all experience hath shown that mankind are more disposed to suffer, while evils are sufferable, than to right themselves by abolishing the forms to which they are accustomed. But when a long train of abuses and usurpations, pursuing invariably the same object, evinces a design to reduce them under absolute despotism, it is their right, it is their duty, to throw off such government, and to provide new guards for their future security. Such has been the patient sufferance of these colonies; and such is now the necessity which constrains them to alter their former systems of government. The history of the present king of Great Britain is a history of repeated injuries and usurpations, all having in direct object the establishment of an absolute tyranny over these states. To prove this, let facts be submitted to a candid world.

He has refused his assent to laws, the most wholesome and necessary for the public good.

He has forbidden his governors to pass laws of immediate and pressing importance, unless suspended in their operation till his assent should be obtained; and, when so suspended, he has utterly neglected to attend to them.

He has refused to pass other laws for the accommodation of large districts of people, unless those people would relinquish the right of representation in the legislature—a right inestimable to them, and formidable to tyrants only.

He has called together legislative bodies at places unusual, uncomfortable, and distant from the depository of their public records, for the sole purpose of fatiguing them into compliance with his measures.

He has dissolved representative houses repeatedly for opposing, with manly firmness, his invasions on the rights of the people.

He has refused for a long time, after such dissolutions, to cause others to be elected; whereby the legislative powers, incapable of annihilation, have returned to the people at large for their exercise; the State remaining, in the meantime, exposed to all the dangers of invasions from without and convulsions within.

He has endeavored to prevent the population of these States; for that purpose obstructing the laws for naturalization of foreigners; refusing to pass others to encourage their migration hither, and raising the conditions of new appropriations of lands.

He has obstructed the administration of justice by refusing his assent to laws for establishing judiciary powers.

He has made judges dependent on his will alone for the tenure of their offices and the amount and payment of their salaries.

He has erected a multitude of new offices, and sent hither swarms of officers to harass our people and eat out their substance.

He has kept among us, in times of peace, standing armies, without the consent of our legislatures.

He has affected to render the military independent of, and superior to, the civil power.

He has combined with others to subject us to a jurisdiction foreign to our Constitution and unacknowledged by our laws, giving his assent to their acts of pretended legislation:

For quartering large bodies of armed troops among us;

For protecting them, by a mock trial, from punishment for any murders which they should commit on the inhabitants of these States;

For cutting off our trade with all parts of the world;

For imposing taxes on us without our consent;

For depriving us, in many cases, of the benefits of trial by jury;

For transporting us beyond seas to be tried for pretended offenses;

For abolishing the free system of English laws in a neighboring province, establishing therein an arbitrary government, and enlarging its boundaries so as to render it at once an example and fit instrument for introducing the same absolute rule into these colonies;

For taking away our charters, abolishing our most valuable laws, and altering fundamentally the forms of our governments;

For suspending our own legislatures and declaring themselves invested with power to legislate for us in all cases whatsoever.

He has abdicated government here by declaring us out of his protection and waging war against us.

He has plundered our seas, ravaged our coasts, burnt our towns, and destroyed the lives of our people.

He is at this time transporting large armies of foreign mercenaries to complete the works of death, desolation, and tyranny, already begun with circumstances of cruelty and perfidy scarcely paralleled in the most barbarous ages, and totally unworthy the head of a civilized nation.

He has constrained our fellow-citizens, taken captive on the high seas, to bear arms against their country, to become the executioners of their friends and brethren, or to fall themselves by their hands.

He has excited domestic insurrections amongst us, and has endeavored to bring on the inhabitants of our frontiers the merciless Indian savages, whose known rule of warfare is an undistinguished destruction of all ages, sexes, and conditions.

In every stage of these oppressions we have petitioned for redress in the most humble terms; our repeated petitions have been answered only by repeated injury. A prince, whose character is thus marked by every act which may define a tyrant, is unfit to be the ruler of a free people.

Nor have we been wanting in our attentions to our British brethren. We have warned them, from time to time, of attempts by their legislature to extend an unwarrantable jurisdiction over us. We have reminded them of the circumstances of our emigration and settlement here. We have appealed to their native justice and magnanimity, and we have conjured them by the ties of our common kindred to disavow these usurpations, which would inevitably interrupt our connections and correspondence. They, too, have been deaf to the voice of justice and of consanguinity. We must, therefore, acquiesce in the necessity which denounces our separation, and hold them, as we hold the rest of mankind,—enemies in war; in peace, friends.

We, therefore, the representatives of the United States of America, in general Congress assembled, appealing to the Supreme Judge of the world for the rectitude of our intentions, do, in the name and by authority of the good people of these colonies, solemnly publish and declare that these united Colonies are, and of right ought to be, free and independent states; that they are absolved from all allegiance to the British crown, and that all political connection between them and the state of Great Britain is, and ought to be, totally dissolved; and that, as free and independent states, they have full power to levy war, conclude peace, contract alliances, establish commerce, and do all other acts and things which independent states may of right do. And, for the support of this Declaration, with a firm reliance on the protection of Divine Providence, we mutually pledge to each other our lives, our fortunes, and our sacred honor.

THE GLAD TIDINGS ARE SPREAD

While the vote on the adoption of the Declaration of Independence was being taken in the State House at Philadelphia, crowds surged about the streets. The suspense was terrible. Would the Congress dare declare the colonies free? Would they dare defy the power of England?

The old State House bell was to ring out the news if Congress adopted the Declaration. Already, in the belfry, the old bell-ringer waited for the signal. At last it came, and as his grandson bounded up the stairs shouting, "Ring! Ring! Ring!" the peals of the bell broke forth, spreading the good news far and near. And the shouts from the crowds below told that the joyous sound found echo in the hearts of the people of the new and independent nation.

INDEPENDENCE BELL

AUTHOR UNKNOWN

There was tumult in the city,
   In the quaint old Quaker town,
And the streets were rife with people
   Pacing restless up and down,—
People gathering at corners,
   Where they whispered each to each,
And the sweat stood on their temples
   With the earnestness of speech.

INDEPENDENCE HALL, PHILADELPHIA

In Independence Hall the Second Continental Congress met and declared war on England, George Washington was appointed commander-in-chief of the Colonial army, and the Declaration of Independence was signed.

As the bleak Atlantic currents
  Lash the wild Newfoundland shore,
So they beat against the State House,
  So they surged against the door;
And the mingling of their voices
  Made a harmony profound,
Till the quiet street of Chestnut
  Was all turbulent with sound.

"Will they do it?" "Dare they do it?"
  "Who is speaking?" "What's the news?"
"What of Adams?" "What of Sherman?"
  "Oh, God grant they won't refuse!"
"Make some way there!" "Let me nearer!"
  "I am stifling!" "Stifle then!
When a nation's life's at hazard,
  We've no time to think of men!"

So they beat against the portal,
  Man and woman, maid and child;
And the July sun in heaven
  On the scene looked down and smiled:
The same sun that saw the Spartan
  Shed his patriot blood in vain
Now beheld the soul of freedom,
  All unconquered, rise again.

See! See! The dense crowd quivers
  Through all its lengthy line,
As the boy beside the portal
  Looks forth to give the sign!

THE LIBERTY BELL SPREADS THE JOYOUS NEWS

Aloft in the tower of the State House in Philadelphia the old bell-ringer awaited word that the Continental Congress had signed the Declaration of Independence. At last it came, and the bell rang out the glad tidings.

With his little hands uplifted,
    Breezes dallying with his hair,
Hark! with deep, clear intonation,
    Breaks his young voice on the air.

Hushed the people's swelling murmur,
  List the boy's exultant cry!
"Ring!" he shouts, "Ring! Grandpa,
  Ring! oh, ring for Liberty!"
Quickly at the given signal
  The old bell-man lifts his hand,
Forth he sends the good news, making
  Iron music through the land.

How they shouted! What rejoicing!
  How the old bell shook the air,
Till the clang of freedom ruffled
  The calmly gliding Delaware!
How the bonfires and the torches
  Lighted up the night's repose,
And from the flames, like fabled Phoenix,
  Our glorious Liberty arose!

That old State House bell is silent,
  Hushed is now its clamorous tongue;
But the spirit it awakened
  Still is living—ever young;
And when we greet the smiling sunlight
  On the Fourth of each July,
We will ne'er forget the bell-man
  Who, betwixt the earth and sky,
Rung out, loudly, "Independence";
  Which, please God, shall never die!

JOHN ADAMS SPEAKS THROUGH
DANIEL WEBSTER

John Adams of Massachusetts was the champion of liberty in the northern colonies as Patrick Henry was in the south. He was on the committee which drew up the Declaration of Independence, and he fought with all his zeal to have it adopted.

The great speech which expressed the conviction of John Adams on the adoption of the Declaration of Independence was not made until after Adams was dead. Daniel Webster made it in a Fourth of July oration in memory of Adams and Jefferson. The speech begins with the ringing words which have inspired patriots ever since: "Sink or swim, live or die, survive or perish, I give my hand and my heart to this vote."

Webster, a greater orator than Adams, though not a greater patriot, recited the speech as having heard it from Adams' lips. But in truth, only the ideas had come from Adams. Webster called to life the spirit of the great patriot, and put these noble words into his mouth.

He pictured him standing there in Independence Hall with the great issue before him: Should the American colonists be safe and dependent, or should they risk their necks on the chance of winning freedom for themselves and for the America of the future?

"SINK OR SWIM"

DANIEL WEBSTER

Sink or swim, live or die, survive or perish, I give my hand and my heart to this vote. It is true, indeed, that in the beginning we aimed not at independence. But there is a Divinity which shapes our ends.

The injustice of England has driven us to arms; and, blinded to her own interest, she has obstinately persisted, till independence is now within our grasp. We have but to reach forth to it, and it is ours.

Why, then, should we defer the Declaration? Is any man so weak as now to hope for a reconciliation with England, which shall leave either safety to the country and its liberties, or safety to his own life and his own honor?

Are not you, sir, who sit in that chair,—is not he, our venerable colleague near you,—are you not both already the proscribed and predestined objects of punishment and of vengeance? Cut off from all hope of royal clemency, what are you, what can you be, while the power of England remains, but outlaws?

If we postpone independence, do we mean to carry on, or to give up, the war? Do we mean to submit to the measures of Parliament, Boston Port Bill and all? Do we mean to submit, and consent that we ourselves shall be ground to powder and our country and its rights trodden down in the dust? I

JOHN ADAMS

A courageous, far-seeing patriot, John Adams of Massachusetts
was one of the first to urge the colonies to separate from England.

know we do not mean to submit. We never shall submit.

Do we intend to violate that most solemn obligation ever entered into by men—that plighting, before God, of our sacred honor to Washington, when, putting him forth to incur the dangers of war, as well as the political hazards of the times, we promised to adhere to him, in every extremity, with our fortunes and our lives? I know there is not a man here who would not rather see a general conflagration sweep over the land, or an earthquake sink it, than one jot or tittle of that plighted faith fall to the ground.

For myself, having twelve months ago in this place moved you that George Washington be appointed commander of the forces, raised or to be raised, for defense of American liberty, may my right hand forget its cunning, and my tongue cleave to the roof of my mouth, if I hesitate or waver in the support I give him.

The war, then, must go on. We must fight it through. And, if the war must go on, why put off longer the Declaration of Independence? That measure will strengthen us. It will give us character abroad. The nations will then treat with us, which they never can do while we acknowledge ourselves subjects in arms against our sovereign.

Nay, I maintain that England herself will sooner treat for peace with us on the footing of independence, than consent, by repealing her acts, to acknowledge that her whole conduct towards us has been a course of injustice and oppression. Her pride will be less wounded by submitting to that course of things which now predestinates our independence, than by yielding the points in controversy to her rebellious subjects. The former she would regard as the result of fortune; the latter she would feel as her own deep disgrace.

Why, then—why, then, sir, do we not, as soon as possible, change this from a civil to a national war? And since we must fight it through, why not put ourselves in a state to enjoy all the benefits of victory, if we gain the victory?

If we fail, it can be no worse for us. But we shall not fail. The cause will raise up armies; the cause will create navies. The people—the people, if we are true to them, will carry us, and will carry themselves, gloriously through this struggle. I care not how fickle other people have been found. I know the people of these colonies, and I know that resistance to British aggression is deep and settled in their hearts and cannot be eradicated. Every colony, indeed, has expressed its willingness to follow, if we but take the lead.

Sir, the Declaration will inspire the people with increased courage. Instead of a long and bloody war for restoration of privileges, for redress of grievances, for chartered immunities, held under a British king, set before them the glorious object of entire independence, and it will breathe into them anew the breath of life.

Read this Declaration at the head of the army; every sword will be drawn from its scabbard, and the solemn vow uttered to maintain it, or to perish on the bed of honor. Publish it from the pulpit; religion will approve it, and the love of religious liberty will cling round it, resolved to stand with it, or fall with it. Send it to the public halls; proclaim it there; let them hear it, who heard the first roar of the enemy's cannon; let them see it, who saw their brothers and their sons fall on the field of Bunker Hill, and in the streets of Lexington and Concord, and the very walls will cry out in its support.

Sir, I know the uncertainty of human affairs, but I see, I see clearly, through this day's business. You and I, indeed, may rue it. We may not live to the time when this Declaration shall be made good. We may die; die, colonists; die, slaves; die, it may be, ignominiously and on the scaffold. Be it so. Be it so. If it be the pleasure of Heaven that my country shall require the poor offering of my life, the victim shall be ready at the appointed hour of sacrifice, come when that hour may. But while I do live, let me have a country, or at least the hope of a country, and that a free country.

But, whatever may be our fate, be assured, be assured, that this Declaration will stand. It may cost treasure, and it may cost blood; but it will stand, and it will richly compensate for both. Through the thick gloom of the present I see the brightness of the future as the sun in heaven. We shall make this a glorious,

an immortal day.   When we are in our graves, our
children will honor it.   They will celebrate it with
thanksgiving, with festivity, with bonfires, and illumi-
nations.   On its annual return they will shed tears,
copious, gushing tears, not of subjection and slavery,
not of agony and distress, but of exultation, of gratitude, and of joy.

Sir, before God, I believe the hour has come.   My
judgment approves this measure, and my whole
heart is in it.   All that I have, and all that I am, and
all that I hope, in this life, I am now ready here to
stake upon it; and I leave off as I began, that, live
or die, survive or perish, I am for the Declaration.
It is my living sentiment, and, by the blessing of
God, it shall be my dying sentiment; independence
now, and independence forever.

Brown Brothers, N. Y.

BETSY ROSS AND THE FIRST AMERICAN FLAG

Betsy Ross proudly shows the first American flag to General Washington. So well did Congress like her work that she was given the task of making all the government flags.

THE STARS AND STRIPES

The story has come down to us that Mrs. Betsy Ross, of Philadelphia, made the flag which Congress adopted as the national emblem of union and independence on June 14, 1777, by the act: "Resolved, that the flag of the thirteen United States shall be thirteen stripes, alternate red and white, and that the Union be thirteen white stars on a blue field."

The only difference between the flag of 1777 and our flag of today is in the number and arrangement of the stars. The original flag had thirteen stars, one star for each state, in the form of a circle. Today, the forty-eight stars, also one star for each state, are in six rows of eight stars each.

Each time a state has been admitted to the Union, a star has been added to our flag. The addition of stars, one by one, represents the growth of our country. Since we love our country for what it is and for what it stands, we love and respect our flag, the emblem which represents union and the liberty which we enjoy.

THE FLAG GOES BY

HENRY HOLCOMB BENNETT

Hats off!
Along the street there comes
A blare of bugles, a ruffle of drums,
A flash of color beneath the sky.
Hats off!
The flag is passing by!

Blue, and crimson, and white it shines,
Over the steel-tipped, ordered lines.
Hats off!
The colors before us fly;
But more than the flag is passing by.

Sea fights and land fights, grim and great,
Fought to make and to save the State;

Weary marches and sinking ships;
Cheers of victory on dying lips;

Days of plenty, and years of peace,
March of a strong land's swift increase;
Equal justice, right, and law,
Stately honor and reverend awe;

Sign of a Nation, great and strong,
To ward her people from foreign wrong;
Pride, and glory, and honor, all
Live in the colors to stand or fall.

Hats off!
Along the street there comes
A blare of bugles, a ruffle of drums;
And loyal hearts are beating high.
Hats off!
The flag is passing by!

BENJAMIN FRANKLIN

Patriot, statesman, author, scientist, and inventor, Franklin was the spokesman of the colonies for many years. When the government of the United States was framed, his wisdom and tolerance helped to settle many troublesome questions.

FRAMING THE GOVERNMENT FOR OUR NATION

THE DRAFTING OF OUR CONSTITUTION

During most of the Revolutionary War, our country was governed by the Second Continental Congress. This Congress had no definite powers, but at a time when the country was fighting for its very life, many things had to be done and done quickly. There was no time to wait for each state to agree or disagree, and the Congress made the decisions and acted on them.

Realizing that a Congress without power could not carry on indefinitely, the representatives drew up, in 1776, a constitution known as the Articles of Confederation. Some of the states adopted the new constitution promptly, but some did not, and even after they had all adopted it the Articles of Confederation proved to be very lacking. They gave Congress too little power and the states too much. Foreign countries would not deal with so weak a government. There were bitter jealousies between the states. Plainly some stronger form of government was needed if the United States were to remain a united nation.

In 1787 a meeting was held in Philadelphia to

revise and strengthen the Articles. It was soon clear, however, that they were too weak to form even the basis of a government, and the delegates to the convention decided to build a new constitution.

All through the hot summer of 1787 the men at Philadelphia worked behind closed doors to give our country the new and better constitution it needed. Many and bitter were the quarrels which threatened to undo their work and split our country into thirteen jealous and wrangling little nations. Often Washington, Franklin, and other leaders urged the angry delegates to compromise and to work out peacefully the troublesome problems which seemed to have no possible solution. Wisdom and patience prevailed; by the end of summer the work of building the Constitution of the United States was done.

THE FRAMEWORK OF OUR CONSTITUTION

Every American should be familiar with the Constitution of the United States, for this great document not only regulates the running of our national government but also guarantees the liberties which we love so much.

The first fifty-two words of the Constitution— the preamble—set forth the reasons for drawing up this new and different form of government, as follows:

"We, the people of the United States, in order to form a more perfect union, establish justice, insure domestic tranquility, provide for the common defense, promote the general welfare, and secure the blessings of liberty to ourselves and our posterity, do ordain and establish this Constitution for the United States of America."

Article I sets forth the powers and the procedure to be followed by the Legislative Branch of the government, which is called Congress.

Article II describes the powers and duties of the Executive Department, which consists of the President, the Vice-President, and the members of the President's Cabinet. The Constitution does not call them Cabinet members; it speaks of them as "heads of departments." This article also tells how the President and the Vice-President shall be elected.

Article III gives the powers of the Judicial Department, which includes the Supreme Court and the lesser courts which try government cases.

Article IV guarantees the citizens of all states the same privileges under the national government, and sets forth what shall be the relation of one state to the others and of the United States government to the states.

Article V describes the manner in which the Constitution may be amended.

Article VI states that all bills owed by the government before the adoption of the Constitution should be paid, that the Constitution and all laws based upon it shall be the law of the land, and that all government officers, state and national, shall be required to take an oath to support the Constitution, but that they will never be required to take a religious test of any kind.

Article VII says that the vote of nine states (of the thirteen) shall be enough to ratify the Constitution.

The complete text of the Constitution of the United States will be found on pages *1* to *23* in the APPENDIX.

ADOPTION OF THE CONSTITUTION

When at last the Constitution was completed, it was submitted to the members of the convention for their signatures. Delegate after delegate raised objections, for they did not agree on all the proposed laws. It looked as if all the work had been for nothing.

Then Benjamin Franklin, who represented Pennsylvania at the convention, delivered a speech arguing for its adoption. So well did he make his points that, one by one, the majority of the delegates signed the Constitution, and it was ready to be ratified by the various states.

FRANKLIN URGES THE ADOPTION OF THE CONSTITUTION

At the Constitutional Convention, Philadelphia, 1787.

I confess that I do not entirely approve of this Constitution at present; but sir, I am not sure I shall never approve it, for, having lived long, I have experienced many instances of being obliged, by better information or fuller consideration, to change opinions even on important subjects, which I once thought right, but found to be otherwise. It is therefore that, the older I grow, the more apt I am to doubt my own judgment of others.

Most men, indeed, as well as most sects in religion,

think themselves in possession of all truth, and that wherever others differ from them it is so far error. . . .

But, though many private persons think almost as highly of their own infallibility as of that of their sect, few express it so naturally as a certain French lady, who, in a little dispute with her sister, said: "But I meet with nobody but myself that is always in the right."

In these sentiments, sir, I agree to this Constitution, with all its faults,—if they are such,—because I think a general government necessary for us, and there is no form of government but what may be a blessing to the people, if well administered; and I believe, further, that this is likely to be well administered for a course of years, and can only end in despotism, as other forms have done before it, when the people shall become so corrupted as to need despotic government, being incapable of any other.

I doubt, too, whether any other convention we can obtain may be able to make a better Constitution; for, when you assemble a number of men, to have the advantage of their joint wisdom, you inevitably assemble with those men all their prejudices, their passions, their errors of opinion, their local interests, and their selfish views. From such an assembly can a perfect production be expected?

It therefore astonishes me, sir, to find this system approaching so near to perfection as it does; and I think it will astonish our enemies, who are waiting

with confidence to hear that our counsels are con-
founded like those of the builders of Babel, and that
our States are on the point of separation, only to meet
hereafter for the purpose of cutting one another's
throats.

Thus I consent, sir, to this Constitution, because
I expect no better, and because I am not sure that it
is not the best. The opinions I have had of its errors
I sacrifice to the public good. I have never whispered
a syllable of them abroad. Within these walls they
were born, and here they shall die.

If every one of us, in returning to our constituents,
were to report the objections he has had to it, and
endeavor to gain partisans in support of them, we
might prevent its being generally received, and
thereby lose all the salutary effects and great advan-
tages resulting naturally in our favor among foreign
nations, as well as among ourselves, from our real or
apparent unanimity.

Much of the strength and efficiency of any government, in procuring and securing happiness to the
people, depends on opinion, on the general opinion
of the goodness of that government, as well as of the
wisdom and integrity of its governors. I hope, therefore, for our own sakes, as a part of the people, and
for the sake of our posterity, that we shall act heartily
and unanimously in recommending this Constitution
wherever our influence may extend, and turn our
future thoughts and endeavors to the means of having
it well administered.

On the whole, sir, I cannot help expressing a wish that every member of the convention who may still have objection to it, would, with me, on this occasion, doubt a little of his own infallibility, and, to make manifest our unanimity, put his name to this instrument.

AMENDMENTS TO THE CONSTITUTION

Because the Constitution did not definitely name the rights for which they had fought so hard, some of the states refused to adopt it unless those rights were made a part of it. The states were given the promise that the rights which they prized so highly would be added to the Constitution at the earliest possible moment. Because of this promise, ten states, one more than the required number, had ratified the Constitution by the end of June, 1788, and it became the law of the United States.

The first Congress under the new government soon framed ten amendments to the Constitution. These ten amendments have been called the Bill of Rights because they set forth the rights and privileges the people of the country felt they should have guaranteed to them. When, in 1791, the states had approved the Bill of Rights it became a part of the Constitution.

It is a splendid tribute to the foresight and wisdom of the delegates to the Constitutional Convention that the document they framed in 1787 has since then been modified only twenty-one times including the ten amendments of the Bill of Rights.

The text of the twenty-one amendments to the Constitution will be found on pages *15* to *23* of the APPENDIX.

THE STRUGGLES OF THE NEW NATION

WASHINGTON AND HIS "FAREWELL ADDRESS"

The Revolutionary War, under the brilliant direction of George Washington, had been won; and with its conclusion the freedom of our country from the rule of England was an established fact.

Washington, weary from the weight of responsibility and the severe campaigns of the war, had retired to the peace and quiet of his beautiful estate at Mount Vernon, Virginia. It was no life of ease to which he intended to settle down, for there was much to be done in building up his plantation to its former excellence, since the estate showed the effects of the master's absence during the years of the war.

Though it was Washington's wish to return to private life, his home state of Virginia felt that the country still needed him. He was persuaded to represent Virginia at the Constitutional Convention which met at Philadelphia in 1787 to frame the Constitution. The members of that body chose him to preside over the work, and it was largely through his untiring efforts that the document was finally drafted. When it was completed, he was the first to sign, which influenced others to follow his example.

American Historical Bureau, N. Y.

MOUNT VERNON

George Washington's beautiful colonial home, overlooking the Potomac River, is one of America's most honored shrines.

Appropriate as was the selection of Washington to preside over the Constitutional Convention, even more appropriate was his election as first President of the United States. Wisdom, judgment, vision, and understanding were needed in putting into operation the new and untried government. Washington possessed those qualities, and fortunate indeed was the young nation to have so able a leader to guide it through the trying years of its beginning.

As President of the United States, eight more years of unselfish devotion to his country were added to Washington's long period of public life. Near the close of his second presidential term, Washington made it clear that he was now determined to spend the remainder of his life as a private citizen. A message to this effect, intended for the people of the country, was delivered before the Senate and the House of Representatives on September 17, 1796.

The message in which Washington announced his retirement from public life is called his "Farewell Address." It is one of the greatest of American speeches, but it is much more than a speech. In it are many of the wisest pieces of advice ever given a nation, advice which is just as good today as it was in the days when it was given.

In his "Farewell Address" Washington particularly urged: that the Union of the states be protected from any sectional political parties, such as Northern, Southern, Atlantic, or Western, which would cause the people of different parts of the country to feel that their interests were not the same; that education be encouraged; that a large army in time of peace be discouraged as dangerous to liberty; that the departments of government be kept separate and that too much power be not given to one department since this might be at the expense of the others; that to spend money to avoid danger is often less expensive than to wait until the danger appears; that a large public debt be avoided; that the country be kept politically independent of all foreign nations. This excellent advice which Washington as an "old and affectionate friend" gave his country was invaluable to the young nation struggling through its early years.

So great and so many were the democratic services rendered by Washington that he is very properly called the "father of his country," and is paid the tribute of having been "first in war, first in peace, and first in the hearts of his countrymen."

Sections from the text of Washington's "Farewell Address" will be found on pages *24* to *31* of the APPENDIX.

CHARLES COTESWORTH PINCKNEY

The spirit of American independence was sounded by Charles Pinckney, our ambassador to France, when French agents demanded that our country pay to keep out of war. "Millions for defense! Not one cent for tribute!" Pinckney answered.

OUR NATION NOT FOR SALE

Charles Cotesworth Pinckney would be worthy of a place in the honor roll of patriots who fought for our country's freedom and for democracy if he had done nothing besides insist that there be placed in our Constitution the clause, "No religious test shall ever be required as a qualification to any office or public trust under the United States." But Charles Pinckney should be honored also for the stand he took on another question.

In 1793, France and England were at war, and each country was anxious to have the United States enter the conflict on its side. But our country declared that it would remain neutral. This enraged both France and England, and they began to seize American ships on the high seas.

In 1796, Pinckney went to France to take over the office of United States minister. The government of France not only refused to see him, but ordered him to leave the country. When news of this insult reached the United States, President John Adams called a special session of Congress and urged that a firm stand be taken.

It was decided to send John Marshall and Elbridge Gerry to join Pinckney, who was then in Holland. Instead of receiving the United States representatives personally, the French minister sent three agents to deal with them. These agents told the Americans

that war could be avoided if the United States would
lend France money to carry on her war with England
and if large sums of money were paid to a few important men in the French government.   Upon hearing
these proposals, Pinckney is said to have exclaimed,
"Millions for defense! Not one cent for tribute!"

Feeling in the United States rose to a high pitch
when the American ambassadors returned with their
report.   Pinckney's words became a popular slogan.
George Washington was recalled from retirement to
again command the army; Congress created the Navy
Department; and the United States prepared to go
to war with France.   Though war was not actually
declared, the United States Navy during the next two
years captured eighty French ships.

When Napoleon Bonaparte came to power in
France in 1799, he had enough to do to straighten out
affairs at home without having difficulties abroad, so
he soon made a treaty satisfactory to the United
States.   Thus the situation created by the refusal of
the French government to receive Pinckney as minister from the United States was ended.

"Millions for defense!   Not one cent for tribute!"
expressing as it did the attitude of our country and
the stand she took in a crisis, has represented throughout all the years of our history the spirit of a free
people.   Since the days of Charles Cotesworth Pinckney, the foreign envoys of the United States have
been treated with the respect which is due them.

NATIONAL UNITY IS STRENGTHENED

In times of national peril it is of the greatest importance that the people of a country be united in the
common cause, that they be "as a band of brothers
joined." Such a time faced our country in the troublous
days of threatened war with France. The noble words of
the song "Hail, Columbia!" written in 1798, voiced the
feeling of every true citizen of our land during those dark
and uncertain days.

HAIL, COLUMBIA!

JOSEPH HOPKINSON

Hail! Columbia, happy land!
Hail! ye heroes, heaven-born band,
Who fought and bled in freedom's cause,
Who fought and bled in freedom's cause,
And when the storm of war was gone,
Enjoyed the peace your valor won;
Let independence be your boast,
Ever mindful what it cost,
Ever grateful for the prize,
Let its altar reach the skies.

Firm, united let us be,
Rallying round our liberty,
As a band of brothers joined,
Peace and safety we shall find.

Immortal patriots, rise once more!
Defend your rights, defend your shore;
Let no rude foe, with impious hand,
Let no rude foe with impious hand
Invade the shrine where sacred lies
Of toil and blood the well-earned prize;
While offering peace, sincere and just,
In Heaven we place a manly trust,
That truth and justice may prevail,
And every scheme of bondage fail.

Sound, sound the trump of fame!
Let Washington's great name
Ring through the world with loud applause!
Ring through the world with loud applause!
Let every clime to freedom dear
Listen with a joyful ear;
With equal skill, with steady power,
He governs in the fearful hour
Of horrid war, or guides with ease
The happier time of honest peace.

Behold the chief, who now commands,
Once more to serve his country stands
The rock on which the storm will beat!
The rock on which the storm will beat!
But, armed in virtue, firm and true,
His hopes are fixed on Heaven and you.

When hope was sinking in dismay,
When gloom obscured Columbia's day,
His steady mind, from changes free,
Resolved on death or liberty.

> Firm, united let us be
> Rallying round our liberty,
> As a band of brothers joined,
> Peace and safety we shall find.

THOMAS JEFFERSON

Today, as nearly a century and a half ago, Thomas Jefferson is a symbol of all that is truly democratic. He had an unwavering trust in the ability of the people to exercise the power of self-government which the Constitution gave them.

THOMAS JEFFERSON, A TRUE DEMOCRAT

The period which immediately preceded the election of Thomas Jefferson as third President of the United States, in 1800, was one of the most critical in the history of our country from the standpoint of "liberty and justice for all."

At that time the national government was being carried on by the Federalist party. Although the Federalists had done much towards establishing our government on a firm and sane basis, they believed that the central government should have much more power than was granted it by the Constitution, and they wanted the government's policies decided by a few educated men. The Democratic-Republican party, of which Thomas Jefferson was the leader, was opposed to these ideas. It stood strongly for government by the people and did not want to see the powers of the states taken over by the central government.

In 1798 the Federalists passed a law which many people thought was unconstitutional. Our country had refused to take sides with either England or France in their war on each other, and there were many Americans who criticized the government for this action. Strong articles appeared in the newspapers; and, to put a stop to these, Congress passed a law providing for heavy fines and prison sentences for those who published unfriendly criticisms of the government.

This was a blow struck at freedom of speech and freedom of the press, and it aroused people all over the country. So strong was the feeling against the new law that when the next presidential election took place the Federalist candidates were defeated and the Democratic-Republican party was swept into power. Thomas Jefferson was chosen President, and Aaron Burr became Vice-President.

Jefferson's election was a triumph for democracy. He stood solidly for democratic simplicity and the rights of the people. Imagine, if you can, this greatest of democrats, without pomp or ceremony, clad in plain attire, walking unattended down the aisle of the Senate Chamber to take the oath of office. The address which he gave stands as one of the greatest pronouncements of faith in democracy and of determination to further its success that our country possesses.

QUOTATIONS FROM THOMAS JEFFERSON'S FIRST INAUGURAL ADDRESS

. . . Bear in mind this sacred principle: that though the will of the majority is in all cases to prevail, that will, to be rightful, must be reasonable; that the minority possess their equal rights, which equal laws must protect, and to violate which would be oppression. Let us then, fellow-citizens, unite with one heart and one mind, let us restore to social intercourse that harmony and affection without which liberty and even life itself are but dreary things. And let us reflect, that having banished from our land that religious intolerance under which mankind so long bled and suffered, we have yet gained little, if we countenance a political intolerance, as despotic, as wicked, and as capable of as bitter and bloody persecutions. . . .

About to enter, fellow-citizens, upon the exercise of duties which comprehend everything dear and valuable to you, it is proper you should understand what I deem the essential principles of our government, and consequently, those which ought to shape its administration. I will compress them within the narrowest compass they will bear, stating the general principle, but not all its limitations: Equal and exact justice to all men, of whatever state or persuasion, religious or political; peace, commerce, and honest friendship with all nations, entangling alliances with none; the support of the State governments in all their rights, as the most competent administrations for our domestic concerns and the surest bulwarks against anti-republican tendencies; the preservation of the general government in its whole constitutional vigor, as the sheet-anchor of our peace at home and safety abroad; a jealous care of the right of election by the people, a mild and safe corrective of abuses which are lopped by the sword of revolution where peaceable remedies are unprovided; absolute acquiescence in the decisions of the majority, the vital principle of republics, from which there is no appeal but to force, the vital principle and immediate parent of despotism; a well-disciplined militia, our best reliance in peace, and for the first moments of war till regulars may relieve them; the supremacy of the civil over the military authority; economy in the public expense, that labor may be lightly burdened; the honest payment of our debts, and sacred preservation of the public faith; encouragement of agriculture, and of commerce as its handmaid; the diffusion of information, and arraignment of all abuses at the bar of the public reason; freedom of religion, freedom of the press, and freedom of person, under the protection of the *habeas corpus*, and trial by juries impartially selected. These principles form the bright constellation which has gone before us and guided our steps through an age of revolution and reformation. The wisdom of our sages, and blood of our heroes, have been devoted to their attainment; they should be the creed of our political faith, the text of civic instruction, the touchstone by which to try the services of those we trust; and should we wander from them in moments of error or of alarm, let us hasten to retrace our steps, and to regain the road which alone leads to peace, liberty, and safety.

THE UNITED STATES COMPLETES HER INDEPENDENCE

The war between England and France continued through the early years of the nineteenth century. Both countries blockaded each other's ports, and England went so far as to stop and seize vessels leaving American ports if she believed them bound for France. American sailors were taken from the ships by force and compelled to serve in the British navy.

Our government sent strong protests against these acts, but no attention was paid to them. Finally, in 1812, we were forced to go to war with England to insure our freedom of the seas.

The United States had almost no army, and about twenty ships with which to fight England's great navy— the greatest in the world. Nevertheless, in the three years of the war, the little American navy was victorious time and again. For a second time, England learned that Americans were dangerous foes. When peace was finally declared, England acknowledged our right to sail the oceans undisturbed.

The American Revolution gave us freedom of our land. With the close of the War of 1812 we won freedom of the seas and the right to recognition as a world power, a strong and independent nation.

THE FREEDOM OF THE SEAS

FROM A REPORT OF THE COMMITTEE ON FOREIGN RELATIONS
November, 1811

To sum up, in a word, the great cause of complaint against Great Britain, your committee need only say, that the United States, as a sovereign and independent power, claim the right to use the ocean, which is the common and acknowledged highway of nations, for the purposes of transporting, in their own vessels, the products of their own soils and the acquisitions of their own industry to a market in the ports of friendly nations, and to bring home, in return, such articles as their necessities or convenience may require, always regarding the rights of belligerents as defined by the established laws of nations.

Great Britain, in defiance of this incontestable right, captures every American vessel bound to or returning from a port where her commerce is not favored; enslaves our seamen, and, in spite of our remonstrances, perseveres in these aggressions. To wrongs so daring in character and so disgraceful in their execution, it is impossible that the people of the United States should remain indifferent. We must now tamely and quietly submit, or we must resist by those means which God has placed within our reach.

Your committee would not cast a shade over the American name by the expression of a doubt which branch of this alternative will be embraced. The occasion is now presented when the national character, misunderstood and traduced for a time by foreign and domestic enemies, should be vindicated. If we have not rushed to the field of battle like the nations who are led by the mad ambition of a single chief in the avarice of a corrupted court, it has not proceeded from the fear of war, but from our love of justice and humanity.

That proud spirit of liberty and independence which sustained our fathers in the successful assertion of rights against foreign aggression is not yet sunk. The patriotic fire of the Revolution still lives in the American breast with a holy and unextinguishable flame, and will conduct this nation to those high destinies which are not less the reward of dignified moderation than of exalted valor. But we have borne with injury until forbearance has ceased to be a virtue.

The sovereignty and independence of these states, purchased and sanctified by the blood of our fathers, from whom we received them, not for ourselves only, but as the inheritance of our posterity, are deliberately and systematically violated. And the period has arrived when, in the opinion of your committee, it is the sacred duty of Congress to call forth the patriotism and resources of the country. By the aid of these, and with the blessing of God, we confidently trust we shall be able to procure that redress which has been sought for by justice, by remonstrance, and by forbearance in vain.

THE *CONSTITUTION*—*"OLD IRONSIDES"*

This famous wooden man-of-war won the first great sea fight in the War of 1812 against England. Today, repaired and preserved, it stands as a fitting memorial of a proud period in our nation's history.

OUR NAVY IN THE WAR OF 1812

The heroism of our sailors in the War of 1812 is one of the foremost traditions of our navy. Although the American ships were outnumbered fifty to one, their commanders were equal in daring and ability to any in Britain's mighty fleet. Among the famous American warships of that time were the *Constitution* and the *Chesapeake*. In a duel with the British ship *Shannon*, Captain James Lawrence of the *Chesapeake* was mortally wounded. As he was carried below, he commanded his men, "Don't give up the ship." His immortal words today remain one of our navy's chief watchwords.

THE WARSHIP OF 1812

She was no armored cruiser of twice six thousand tons,
With the thirty foot of metal that make your modern
　　guns;
She didn't have a freeboard of thirty foot in clear,
An' she didn't need a million repairin' fund each year.
She had no rackin' engines to ramp an' stamp an'
　　strain,
To work her steel-clad turrets an' break her hull in
　　twain;
She did not have electric lights,—the battle-lantern's
　　glare
Was all the light the 'tween decks had,—an' God's
　　own good fresh air.

She had no gapin' air-flumes to throw us down our
  breath,
An' we didn't batten hatches to smother men to
  death;
She didn't have five hundred smiths—two hundred
  men would do—
In the old-time Yankee frigate for an old-time
  Yankee crew,
An' a fightin' Yankee captain, with his old-time
  Yankee clothes,
A-cursin' Yankee sailors with his old-time Yankee
  oaths.

She was built of Yankee timber and manned by
  Yankee men,
An' fought by Yankee sailors—Lord send their like
  again!
With the wind abaft the quarter and the sea-foam
  flyin' free,
An' every tack and sheet housed taut and braces
  eased to lee,
You could hear the deep sea thunder from the knight-
  heads where it broke,
As she trailed her lee guns under the blindin' whirl
  o' smoke.

She didn't run at twenty knots,—she wasn't built
  to run,—
An' we didn't need a half a watch to handle every
  gun.

Our captain didn't fight his ship from a little pen o'
  steel;
He fought her from his quarter-deck, with two hands
  at the wheel,
An' we fought in Yankee fashion, half-naked,—
  stripped to board,—
An' when they hauled their red flag down we praised
  the Yankee Lord;
We fought like Yankee sailors, an' we'll do it, too,
  again,
You've changed the ships an' methods, but you can't
  change Yankee men!

                              Philadelphia Record

OUR MOST POPULAR NATIONAL ANTHEM

Every true American, when he hears the music of "The Star-Spangled Banner," stands at attention. In poetry and music it is what the flag is in form and color. It represents what our beloved country stands for.

When the words of this song were written, in September, 1814, the war on land had not been going well. Our army was poorly equipped and trained, and had lost a number of important battles in the Northwest. The British had captured our capital city of Washington and burned some of its public buildings. Now they planned to take Baltimore, and laid siege to Fort McHenry, in Baltimore harbor.

Francis Scott Key of Baltimore was a prisoner on a British man-of-war when the attack on the fort began. All day he watched the battle rage and knew that the fort had not been taken. But when darkness came he could not tell its fate, and the anxious hours passed very slowly. At last the dawn broke, and in the first pale light he saw that the Stars and Stripes still waved above the fort, and the British had given up the attack. In his desire to express his joy he wrote on the back of an old letter the words of "The Star-Spangled Banner."

THE STAR-SPANGLED BANNER

Francis Scott Key

Oh, say, can you see, by the dawn's early light,
  What so proudly we hailed at the twilight's last
    gleaming?
Whose broad stripes and bright stars, through the
    perilous fight,
  O'er the ramparts we watched, were so gallantly
    streaming!
And the rockets' red glare, the bombs bursting in
    air,
  Gave proof through the night that our flag was still
    there:
Oh, say, does that star-spangled banner yet wave
  O'er the land of the free and the home of the brave?

On the shore, dimly seen through the mist of the deep,
  Where the foe's haughty host in dread silence
    reposes,
What is that which the breeze o'er the towering
    steep,
  As it fitfully blows, now conceals, now discloses?
Now it catches the gleam of the morning's first
    beam,
  In full glory reflected now shines on the stream:
'Tis the star-spangled banner! Oh long may it wave
  O'er the land of the free and the home of the brave!

And where is that band who so vauntingly swore
  That the havoc of war and the battle's confusion
A home and a country they'd leave us no more?
  Their blood has washed out their foul footsteps'
    pollution.
No refuge could save the hireling and slave
  From terror of flight, or the gloom of the grave:
And the star-spangled banner in triumph doth wave
  O'er the land of the free and the home of the brave!

Oh, thus be it ever, when freemen shall stand
  Between their loved home and the War's deso-
    lation!
Blest with victory and peace, may the Heaven-
    rescued land
  Praise the Power that hath made and preserved
    us a nation.
Then conquer we must, for our cause it is just,
  And this be our motto: "In God is our trust."
And the star-spangled banner in triumph shall wave
  O'er the land of the free and the home of the brave.

THE MONROE DOCTRINE

After the thirteen American colonies had won their fight for freedom and had established an independent union of free states, the spirit of freedom spread to other colonies of the Western Hemisphere. Mexico and Central America, except for the small colony of British Honduras, were under the strict rule of Spain. In South America, Portugal controlled Brazil, while the rest of the continent consisted mainly of Spanish colonies which were ruled by governors from Spain who did not allow the people to have the slightest degree of self-government. Finally, Brazil and all of the Spanish colonies in the New World broke away from foreign control and became independent republics.

Meanwhile, in Europe, a deadly danger raised its head. Four great nations, Prussia, Russia, Austria, and France, united to form the Quadruple Alliance. They had beaten the great Napoleon, and now they set about to restore Europe to its condition before the French Revolution and Napoleon had upset its thrones and boundaries. Spain, who wanted her American colonies restored to her, appealed to the Alliance for help in conquering them.

Both England and the United States were alarmed. The English people feared this powerful Alliance, which might at any moment turn upon them. The people of America feared to have the armies of the Quadruple Alliance so near the borders of the United States. Furthermore, Russia, who owned Alaska, was extending her fishing operations south along the Pacific coast of North America. There was the danger that she might attempt to establish colonies south of Alaska.

This threatened invasion of the Western Hemisphere caused our statesmen to do much serious thinking. England sent a message to President James Monroe suggesting an alliance with her against the four powers. Many of our statesmen favored this suggestion, but John Quincy Adams, Secretary of State, strongly opposed it. He saw too much future danger to the United States in an alliance with England. We were a nation, although not yet a very strong one, and we should settle our own difficulties without placing ourselves under obligations to anyone. We should act alone, boldly and fearlessly. Fortunately Adams' advice was accepted.

On December 2, 1823, President Monroe gave his annual speech to Congress. Naturally much of it dealt with the dangerous foreign situation. Three of his declarations were outstanding: (1) The Americas were not open to further colonization by European powers. This was mainly aimed at Russia. (2) Any effort of the European powers to interfere in the affairs of the Western Hemisphere would be regarded by the United States as a dangerous and unfriendly act. This was a polite way of warning the Quadruple Alliance to leave the former Spanish possessions alone. (3) The United States would not interfere with the internal affairs of any European power.

The Monroe Doctrine, as President Monroe's foreign policy came to be called, has never been made a law. Congress never voted upon it to make it a law. It was never made a part of any treaty. Yet the Monroe Doctrine has played an important part in our history. Because of it, the Quadruple Alliance made no attempt to restore to Spain her former American colonies, and no other nation has tried to plant colonies on American shores. Ever since 1823 we have stood ready to defend our New World neighbors, by force of arms if necessary.

THE AMERICAS FOR AMERICANS

FROM PRESIDENT JAMES MONROE'S ANNUAL MESSAGE TO CONGRESS, DECEMBER 2, 1823.

In the discussion to which this interest has given rise and the arrangements by which they may terminate, the occasion has been judged proper for asserting, as a principle in which the rights and interests of the United States are involved, that the American continents, by the free and independent condition which they have assumed and maintain, are henceforth not to be considered as subjects for future colonization by any European powers. . . .

In the wars of the European powers in matters relating to themselves we have never taken any part, nor does it comport with our policy to do so. It is only when our rights are invaded or seriously menaced that we resent injuries or make preparations for our defense. With the movements in this hemisphere we are of necessity more immediately connected, and by causes which must be obvious to all enlightened and impartial observers. The political system of the allied powers is essentially different in this respect from that of America . . . We owe it, therefore, to candor and to the amicable relations existing between the United States and those powers to declare that we should consider any attempt on their part to extend their system to any portion of this hemisphere as dangerous to our peace and safety. With the existing colonies or dependencies of any European power we have not interfered and shall not interfere. But with the governments who have declared their independence and maintained it, and whose independence we have, on great consideration and on just principles, acknowledged, we could not view any interposition for the purpose of oppressing them, or controlling in any other manner their destiny, by any European power in any other light than as the manifestation of an unfriendly disposition toward the United States. It is impossible that the allied powers should extend their political system to any portion of either continent without endangering our peace and happiness; nor can anyone believe that our southern brethren, if left to themselves, would adopt it of their own accord. It is equally impossible, therefore, that we should behold such interposition in any form with indifference.

THE GREATEST SPEECH OF THE GREATEST AMERICAN ORATOR

Authorities on American history agree that Daniel Webster is probably the greatest orator our country has ever had, and that his speech called the "Reply to Hayne" is his greatest speech.

In 1828, while Daniel Webster was Senator from Massachusetts, the "Tariff of Abominations," as it was called, was passed. This bill placed heavy duties on manufactured cotton and woolen goods imported from abroad. Webster voted for the bill because it protected the manufacturing interests of New England.

The cotton-raising South was bitterly opposed to the tariff. It had been selling its cotton abroad and importing manufactured cotton and woolen goods in return. The duties placed on these goods would raise the prices, and the South felt that this would protect the manufacturers of the North at the expense of the South. Statesmen of South Carolina argued that the tariff law was unconstitutional and that South Carolina could refuse to obey it.

Here was a dangerous idea. If one state could nullify, or set aside, the nation's laws, what would become of the Union? In January, 1830, the whole question of nullification was debated in Congress. Robert Hayne of South Carolina upheld the rights of the states.

Webster replied to Hayne, setting forth in a four-hour speech what he believed our Constitution stands for. He drove home the fact that the Union must come ahead of

DANIEL WEBSTER, A BRILLIANT ORATOR

Webster was a staunch defender of national union and the authority of the Constitution. He devoted most of his life to the service of his country and held the important position of Secretary of State under three Presidents.

the desires of any state, and that the only possible way to preserve our liberty was to uphold the Union. "Liberty and Union, now and forever, one and inseparable!" was his cry.

LIBERTY AND UNION

From Daniel Webster's Reply to Hayne

The people, then, sir, erected this Government. They gave it a Constitution, and in that Constitution they have enumerated the powers which they bestow on it. They have made it a limited Government. They have defined its authority. They have restrained it to the exercise of such powers as are granted; and all others, they declare, are reserved to the States or the people. But, sir, they have not stopped here. If they had, they would have accomplished but half their work. No definition can be so clear as to avoid possibility of doubt; no limitation so precise as to exclude all uncertainty.

Who, then, shall construe this grant of the people? Who shall interpret their will, where it may be supposed they have left it doubtful? With whom do they repose this ultimate right of deciding on the powers of the Government? Sir, they have settled all this in the fullest manner. They have left it with the Government itself, in its appropriate branches.

Sir, the very chief end, the main design, for which the whole Constitution was framed and adopted, was to establish a Government that should not be obliged to act through State agency, or depend on State opinion and State discretion. The people had had quite enough of that kind of Government under the Confederacy. Under that system the legal action —the application of law to individuals—belonged exclusively to the States. Congress could only recommend—their acts were not of binding force till the States had adopted and sanctioned them. Are we in that condition still? Are we yet at the mercy of State discretion and State construction? Sir, if we are, then vain will be our attempt to maintain the Constitution under which we sit.

But, sir, the people have wisely provided in the Constitution itself, a proper, suitable mode and tribunal for settling questions of constitutional law. There are, in the Constitution, grants of powers to Congress, and restrictions on these powers. There are also prohibitions on the States. Some authority must therefore necessarily exist, having the ultimate jurisdiction to fix and ascertain the interpretation of these grants, restrictions, and prohibitions.

The Constitution has itself pointed out, ordained, and established that authority. How has it accomplished this great and essential end? By declaring, sir, that "the Constitution and the laws of the United States, made in pursuance thereof, shall be the supreme law of the land, anything in the Constitution or laws of any State to the contrary notwithstanding."

This, sir, was the first great step. By this the

supremacy of the Constitution and laws of the United States is declared. The people so will it. No State law is to be valid which comes in conflict with the Constitution or any law of the United States passed in pursuance of it. But who shall decide this question of interference? To whom lies the last appeal? This, sir, the Constitution itself decides also by declaring "that the judicial power shall extend to all cases arising under the Constitution and laws of the United States." These two provisions, sir, cover the whole ground. They are in truth the keystone of the arch. With these it is a Constitution; without them it is a Confederacy.

If anything be found in the national Constitution, either by original provision, or subsequent interpretation, which ought not to be in it, the people know how to get rid of it. If any construction be established, unacceptable to them, so as to become, practically, a part of the Constitution, they will amend it, at their own sovereign pleasure; but while the people choose to maintain it, as it is; while they are satisfied with it, and refuse to change it, who has given, or who can give, to the State legislatures a right to alter it, either by interference, construction, or otherwise?

Gentlemen do not seem to recollect that the people have any power to do anything for themselves; they imagine there is no safety for them any longer than they are under the close guardianship of the State legislatures. Sir, the people have not trusted their safety, in regard to the general Constitution, to these hands. They have required other security and taken other bonds. They have chosen to trust themselves, first, to the plain words of the instrument, and to such construction as the Government itself, in doubtful cases, should put on its own powers, under their oaths of office, and subject to their responsibility to them; just as the people of a State trust their own State governments with a similar power.

Secondly, they have reposed their trust in the efficacy of frequent elections, and in their own power to remove their own servants and agents whenever they see cause.

Thirdly, they have reposed trust in the judicial power, which, in order that it might be trustworthy, they have made as respectable, as disinterested, and as independent as was practicable.

Fourthly, they have seen fit to rely in case of necessity, or high expediency, on their known and admitted power, to alter or amend the Constitution, peaceably and quietly, whenever experience shall point out defects or imperfections.

And, finally, the people of the United States have, at no time, in no way, directly or indirectly, authorized any State legislature to construe or interpret their high instrument of government; much less to interfere, by their own power, to arrest its course and operation.

If, sir, the people, in these respects, had done otherwise than they have done, their Constitution could neither have been preserved, nor would it have been worth preserving. And, if its plain provisions shall now be disregarded, and these new doctrines interpolated in it, it will become as feeble and helpless a being as its enemies, whether early or more recent, could possibly desire. It will exist in every State, but as a poor dependent on State permission. It must borrow leave to be and it will be no longer than State pleasure or State discretion sees fit to grant the indulgence and to prolong its poor existence.

But, sir, although there are fears, there are hopes also. The people have preserved this, their own chosen Constitution, for forty years and have seen their happiness, prosperity, and renown grow with its growth, and strengthen with its strength. They are now, generally, strongly attached to it. Overthrown by direct assault, it cannot be; evaded, undermined, nullified, it will not be, if we, and those who shall succeed us here, as agents and representatives of the people, shall conscientiously and vigilantly discharge the two great branches of our public trust— faithfully to preserve and wisely to administer it.

Mr. President, I have thus stated the reasons of my dissent to the doctrines which have been advanced and maintained. I am conscious of having detained you and the Senate much too long. I was drawn into the debate with no previous deliberation such as is suited to the discussion of so grave and important a subject. But it is a subject of which my heart is full, and I have not been willing to suppress the utterance of its spontaneous sentiments. I cannot, even now, persuade myself to relinquish it without expressing once more, my deep conviction, that since it respects nothing less than the Union of the States, it is of most vital and essential importance to the public happiness.

I profess, sir, in my career, hitherto, to have kept steadily in view the prosperity and honor of the whole country and the preservation of our Federal Union. It is to that Union we owe our safety at home and our consideration and dignity abroad. It is to that Union that we are chiefly indebted for whatever makes us most proud of our country. That Union we reached only by the discipline of our virtues in the severe school of adversity. It had its origin in the necessities of disordered finance, prostrate commerce, and ruined credit. Under its benign influence, these great interests immediately awoke as from the dead and sprang forth with newness of life. Every year of its duration has teemed with fresh proofs of its utility and its blessings; and, although our territory has stretched out wider and wider, and our population spread further and further, they have not outrun its protection or its benefits. It has been to us all a copious fountain of national, social, and personal happiness.

I have not allowed myself, sir, to look beyond the Union to see what might lie hidden in the dark recess behind. I have not coolly weighed the chances of preserving liberty when the bonds that unite us together shall be broken asunder. I have not accustomed myself to hang over the precipice of disunion to see whether, with my short sight, I can fathom the depth of the abyss below; nor could I regard him as a safe counselor in the affairs of this Government, whose thoughts should be mainly bent on considering not how the Union should be best preserved, but how tolerable might be the condition of the people when it shall be broken up and destroyed.

While the Union lasts, we have high, exciting, gratifying prospects spread out before us, for us and our children. Beyond that I seek not to penetrate the veil. God grant that in my day, at least, that curtain may not rise. God grant that, on my vision, never may be opened what lies behind.

When my eyes shall be turned to behold, for the last time, the sun in heaven, may I not see him shining on the broken and dishonored fragments of a once glorious Union; on States dissevered, discordant, belligerent; on a land rent with civil feuds, or drenched, it may be, in fraternal blood! Let their last feeble and lingering glance rather behold the gorgeous ensign of the Republic, now known and honored throughout the earth, still full high advanced, its arms and trophies streaming in their original luster, not a stripe erased or polluted, nor a single star obscured, bearing for its motto no such miserable interrogatory as, "What is all this worth?" nor those other words of delusion and folly, "Liberty first and union afterwards"; but everywhere, spread all over in characters of living light, blazing on all its ample folds, as they float over the sea and over the land, and in every wind under the whole heavens, that other sentiment, dear to every true American heart—Liberty and Union, now and forever, one and inseparable!

HENRY WADSWORTH LONGFELLOW

Longfellow is still one of America's best-known and best-loved poets. Some of his more popular poems are "Evangeline," "The Village Blacksmith," "The Wreck of the Hesperus," "The Skeleton in Armor," and "The Courtship of Miles Standish."

LONGFELLOW DESCRIBES THE REPUBLIC

The poem called "The Ship of State" is really part of Longfellow's great poem "The Building of a Ship." It sets forth in different words and in a different form the same belief that Webster had when he said, "It is to that Union we owe our safety at home and our consideration and dignity abroad. It is to that Union that we are chiefly indebted for whatever makes us most proud of our country." And it contains the same thought which Webster expressed, "Liberty and Union, now and forever, one and inseparable!"

THE SHIP OF STATE

HENRY WADSWORTH LONGFELLOW

Thou, too, sail on, O Ship of State!
Sail on, O Union strong and great!
Humanity, with all its fears,
With all the hopes of future years,
Is hanging breathless on thy fate!
We know what Master laid thy keel,
What workmen wrought thy ribs of steel,
Who made each mast and sail and rope,
What anvils rang, what hammers beat,
In what a forge and what a heat
Were shaped the anchors of thy hope!
Fear not each sudden sound and shock,
'Tis of the wave and not the rock;

'Tis but the flapping of the sail,
And not a rent made by the gale!
In spite of rock and tempest's roar,
In spite of false lights on the shore,
Sail on, nor fear to breast the sea!
Our hearts, our hopes, are all with thee,
Our hearts, our hopes, our prayers, our tears,
Our faith triumphant o'er our fears,
Are all with thee,—are all with thee!

THE NATION REJOICES IN SONG

In 1832, "America," our best-known national anthem, written by the Rev. Samuel F. Smith, was sung for the first time at a children's Fourth of July celebration in Boston, Massachusetts. Countless times since then "America" has been sung, and with each singing of its stirring words there has arisen within us a greater love for our "Land of the noble free" and not only the hope that "Long may our land be bright with Freedom's holy light," but an abiding faith that "Freedom's light" shall never grow dim so long as "God speeds our way."

AMERICA

REVEREND SAMUEL F. SMITH

My country, 'tis of thee,
Sweet Land of Liberty,
    Of thee I sing;
Land where my fathers died,
Land of the pilgrims' pride,
From every mountain side
    Let Freedom ring.

My native country, thee,
Land of the noble free,
    Thy name I love;

I love thy rocks and rills,
Thy woods and templed hills;
My heart with rapture thrills
   Like that above.

Let music swell the breeze,
And ring from all the trees
   Sweet Freedom's song;
Let mortal tongues awake;
Let all that breathe partake;
Let rocks their silence break,
   The sound prolong.

Our fathers' God, to Thee,
Author of Liberty,
   To Thee we sing:
Long may our land be bright
With Freedom's holy light;
Protect us by Thy might,
   Great God, our King.

Our glorious Land to-day,
'Neath Education's sway,
   Soars upward still.
Its halls of learning fair,
Whose bounties all may share,
Behold them everywhere
   On vale and hill!

Thy safeguard, Liberty,
The school shall ever be,—
    Our Nation's pride!
No tyrant hand shall smite,
While with encircling might
All here are taught the Right
    With Truth allied.

Beneath Heaven's gracious will
The star of progress still
    Our course doth sway;
In unity sublime
To broader heights we climb,
Triumphant over Time,
    God speeds our way!

Grand birthright of our sires,
Our altars and our fires
    Keep we still pure!
Our starry flag unfurled,
The hope of all the world,
In Peace and Light impearled,
    God hold secure!

PUBLIC EDUCATION AND DEMOCRACY

Hardly had the Puritans settled in Massachusetts before they began to build schools. As early as 1647 a law was passed which required that there should be a free elementary school in every Massachusetts town of fifty or more families and a higher school as well in every town of one hundred or more families. These schools were to be largely paid for by tax money so that everyone should have a share in supporting them.

Usually the elementary schools were small log cabins. In place of desks there was a shelf along the wall, before which the pupils sat on stiff wooden benches. The writing was done on birch-bark with quill pens made from goose feathers. Reading, writing, and arithmetic were about all that were taught, and often the untrained teachers knew little more than their pupils.

In the early years only boys were allowed to attend the schools, but later both girls and boys were admitted to the lower grades. That was all the education girls were supposed to need besides being taught at home to sew, knit, and cook.

Limited as were the schools in Massachusetts, none of the other colonies equalled the Puritan colony in the education of its children, and in some colonies there were no schools at all.

Then came the Revolutionary War, and even in Massachusetts education was neglected. Freedom and independence depended on winning the war, and little else seemed important. After the War was won and the

HORACE MANN, CHAMPION OF PUBLIC EDUCATION

As the first great American crusader for free, tax-supported schools, Horace Mann laid the foundation for public education in the United States. He believed that public education was essential to the success of a democracy.

government of the United States was set up, based on the Constitution, serious thought was again given to education. Was not our country to be governed according to the vote of the people? Then, surely, the people should be educated and intelligent. Moreover, many immigrants were flocking to America, and how could their children become good citizens unless they were given an education? Manufacturing was developing, and to become a valuable worker a man should at least know how to read, write, and cipher. Schools were sorely needed: good schools, paid for by taxation, and open to all children.

So the movement for public education was started, but, as in all movements, a leader was needed to bring together the scattered groups who favored the cause, to act as spokesman, and to devote his time and energy to getting something actually done. And, as in all great movements, a leader appeared. His name was Horace Mann.

Horace Mann was a young lawyer who believed with all his heart that free public education was what America must have. An opportunity to devote himself to this great cause came to him in 1837 when he was appointed secretary of the Massachusetts State Board of Education.

The size of the task which lay before Horace Mann was enough to make even his stout heart tremble. Of existing conditions Mann wrote in his diary, "The laws which sustain our system of common-school instruction are scarcely better than they have been for a century and a half. If schools have improved, it has not been in consequence of any impulse given them by government." Soon after, his diary tells us, "On Friday last, went to Boston where I remained one week. Prepared and issued circulars to the school committees of every town in the State, designating the time and place for holding the proposed conventions in each of the counties. As yet . . . nothing indicates at all in what manner the new mission will be received by the public. All is left for me to do. At the best, perhaps, I can only hope that the community is . . . ready to be swayed one way or the other, according to the manner of putting on the weight."

"All is left for me to do." In that statement there was no shifting of responsibility. Horace Mann was taking upon himself the whole burden. Success or failure depended upon his "manner of putting on the weight," or, in other words, of presenting the justice of his cause so forcefully that the people would be aroused to action.

It was not long before the splendid work and the sincere pleas of Horace Mann began to produce results. In 1839 the first state normal school for the training of teachers was established at Lexington. Of the opening of this school Mann said, "Only three persons presented themselves for examination for the Normal School in Lexington. In point of numbers, this is not a promising commencement. What remains but more exertion, more and more, until it *must* succeed."

So year followed year until 1848, when Mann became a member of Congress from the state of Massachusetts. To him, for his eleven years of unselfish devotion to the cause of public education, our country owes its lasting gratitude. He was public education's first and foremost champion. From the days of Horace Mann the history of public education in the United States has been one of continued growth and improvement.

HORACE MANN, EDUCATOR AND STATESMAN

A speech by Dr. Payson Smith, delivered at Antioch College, Yellow Springs, Ohio, in 1937, at the dedication of the Horace Mann Monument. The dedication marked the centennial anniversary of the beginning of Horace Mann's work in education.

Speech copyrighted by the Antioch Press Company, Yellow Springs, Ohio.

As an introduction to what I have to say, may I ask you to consider the educational scene presented by this country a hundred years ago. The year in which Horace Mann took up his duties as secretary to the Massachusetts State Board of Education was almost exactly two centuries away from three notable events in the history of American education—the founding of the Boston Latin School, the founding of Harvard College, and the promulgation in 1647 of a declaration in behalf of popular education. Eighteen thirty-seven was likewise a half-century away from the time when Washington, Jefferson, and others of the founding Fathers had stated clearly that the education of the people is essential to the security of any government which is based on the principles of democracy.

Notwithstanding these beginnings, it was a sorry condition into which education had declined at the opening of the last century. Neither free public high schools nor higher education had at all generally won the approval and support of the people. By 1830 only three states had established free elementary schools; even in these states, the public schools were usually so inferior that they were patronized only by the children of those who could not afford to pay the tuition charges of private schools. . . . No doubt the grim necessities of those pioneering years, the subduing of the wilderness, and the meagerness of material resources all conspired to prevent the quick fulfillment of those first eager commitments. Whatever the reasons, it was not an attractive educational picture upon which Horace Mann looked a hundred years ago. . . . School buildings and school equipment were meager and shabby. The majority of children attended school irregularly, while many more were in school for extremely limited periods of time, or not at all. The teaching corps was made up of persons whose scholastic equipment was only a little ahead of that of the pupils. Only in the most favored places were children lucky enough to have as teachers young college students preparing for some other profession than teaching, away from their studies for a few weeks in order to get funds to meet their college bills.

But more significant even than these visible deficiencies was the general apathy of the public. With the schools universally poor, there was apparently little discontent about the matter, and no generally expressed desire to correct it. Perhaps no more striking commentary could be found than the disapproval expressed by Mann's friends that he should devote his talents to so mean a task as education.

There must, however, have been deep undercurrents of dissatisfaction among the people that such conditions could exist. Many citizens must have been ready and eager to accept leadership whenever it might appear; otherwise, that leadership could not in the space of twelve years have accomplished such results. Not only was new life infused into the schools, but in reality a national ideal of education was firmly and permanently established. Whatever modification of detail may come, the American people are not likely ever to reject the basic educational philosophy of Horace Mann.

But Mann did not have knowledge and understanding only. He likewise had faith—an essential to the educator and the statesman alike. His faith was of that quality which, not seeing the final goal, yet doubts not what that goal will be. When he dedicated his life and work to posterity he gave expression to a faith that did not falter to the end. . . . Bear in mind that a hundred years ago today there was no such thing anywhere in America as a planned, coherent program of education. A few of the larger towns, to be sure, had several units which might potentially be integrated into systematic organization. Notwithstanding that state constitutions and laws had suggested the state's responsibility for education, and had even in some cases provided warrants for its accomplishment, there was no American state a century ago that had given the practical approval of action to the theories that had been laid down. It is no exaggeration to say that education in this country a hundred years ago today was without order, without defined purpose, and without even the semblance of organized planning.

Certain it is that in America there is nothing today more completely and genuinely American than the American public school. . . . No one now doubts that all children should be assured the privileges of education; no one would now dispute the tenet that society must insure itself through the education of all the people; no one now thinks that education can be made effective without trained teachers; no one today would look upon higher education as the exclusive privilege of men. Yet all of these and many others were controversial questions a century ago. To every one of them Horace Mann brought his sense of justice, his prophetic vision, and his powerful advocacy of the right course as he saw it. It is not to be denied that events favored the rapid extension of the principles for which Mann contended. The opening and settlement of the Northwest Territory, and a little later of the regions of the Far West, led to migrations of the people from the Atlantic seaboard. With them went whatever opinions, convictions, or philosophies they had held.

Horace Mann the educator still lives among us. For nearly twenty years, from the window of my office in the State House at Boston, I could look across the State House grounds. There in the foreground was the statue of a soldier honored for his service on the field of battle. Also there was the statue of one who became a heroic figure in American statesmanship. Beyond these two stood another statue, like the one unveiled here today—the likeness of a man who gave himself to the service of youth. Near that spot he declared that he accepted posterity as his client. Near where we stand today he counseled youth to be ashamed to die until it had won some victory for humanity. These places heard his voice. They knew his presence. What a privilege was theirs! Yet today the circle of his influence is not bounded by the limits of Massachusetts and of Ohio. Wherever teachers teach or children learn, there dwells the spirit of this friend of mankind, statesman and educator, Horace Mann.

ABRAHAM LINCOLN

Through his wisdom, understanding, and patience, Lincoln won for the Union the loyalty of many states which might otherwise have seceded. Though firm in his resolve to preserve the Union, he felt only sympathy and tenderness for the South.

THE WAR BETWEEN THE STATES

THE QUESTION OF HUMAN SLAVERY

Three years before the war between the North and the South, there were no slaves in the North. In all the Southern states there were slaves. When a new state was admitted to the Union, the question at once came up: Shall it be a free state or a slave state? When a slave escaped from a slave state into a free state, the question at once arose: Must the slave be captured in the free state and sent back into slavery?

The country could not agree on these things. In the North, abolitionists, as people who wanted to do away with slave holding were called, were helping slaves to escape and stirring up hatred of slavery through newspaper articles and speeches. The South was bitter over such actions.

Just as Patrick Henry of Virginia, three quarters of a century before, had called upon the Virginia colonists to make up their minds upon the great question of Independence, so Abraham Lincoln, in 1858, told his fellow Americans that the country must make up its mind to be all slave or all free. In his speech Lincoln did not ask that the slaves be freed, but he said that the Union must be preserved and that "a house divided against itself cannot stand."

At the time he made this speech, Lincoln had been nominated Senator for Illinois, but because of his views on slavery he was defeated in the election.

A HOUSE DIVIDED AGAINST ITSELF

Abraham Lincoln

Convention Speech, June 16, 1858

MR. PRESIDENT,
AND GENTLEMEN OF THE CONVENTION:

If we could first know where we are, and whither we are tending, we could better judge what to do, and how to do it. We are now far into the fifth year since a policy was initiated with the avowed object and confident promise of putting an end to slavery agitation. Under the operation of that policy, that agitation has not only not ceased, but has constantly augmented. In my opinion, it will not cease until a crisis shall have been reached and passed.

"A house divided against itself cannot stand." I believe this Government cannot endure permanently half slave and half free. I do not expect the Union to be dissolved,—I do not expect the house to fall,—but I do expect it will cease to be divided. It will become all one thing or all the other. Either the opponents of slavery will arrest the further spread of it, and place it where the public mind shall rest in the belief that it is in the course of ultimate extinction; or its advocates will push it forward, till it shall become alike lawful in all the States, old as well as new—North as well as South.

LINCOLN DURING THE WAR BETWEEN THE STATES

Although Abraham Lincoln lost the election to the Senate in 1858, he was elected, two years later, to the Presidency of the United States. Hardly had his term begun when war broke out between the North and the South. Seven Southern states had seceded and set up a separate government called the Confederate States of America. The Confederates in Charleston, South Carolina, fired on Fort Sumter, the Union fort in the harbor; and on April 15, 1861, Lincoln called for troops to preserve the Union.

At once both sides prepared for war. Four more states left the Union and joined the Confederacy. In the North, even Lincoln's bitterest enemies flocked to his support.

At first the Union army proved unequal to its task. Its commanders were too cautious and time and again lost the opportunity of trapping the Confederate forces. On the other hand, the Union navy succeeded in blocking the Southern ports, which worked a hardship on the people of the South. Then, on January 1, 1863, Lincoln proclaimed that all slaves in the seceded states should be free, and many of them fled to the North. This was a blow to the South for it took away slave labor needed to raise crops.

In the summer of 1863 the Southern armies invaded the North. At Gettysburg, Pennsylvania, a great battle was fought. In this battle the Union armies were victorious. Thousands of Confederates lost their lives, and many Union soldiers fell. In November of that year, at the dedication of the cemetery at Gettysburg where soldiers of both sides lay buried, Lincoln made a speech which is one of the great orations of the English language. In it he showed no bitterness toward the South, only a great compassion for those who had died in the struggle, and a hope that the nation would be preserved.

LINCOLN'S GETTYSBURG ADDRESS
November 19, 1863

Fourscore and seven years ago, our fathers brought forth on this continent a new nation, conceived in liberty, and dedicated to the proposition that all men are created equal. Now we are engaged in a great civil war, testing whether that nation, or any nation so conceived and so dedicated, can long endure. We are met on a great battlefield of that war. We have come to dedicate a portion of that field as a final resting-place for those who here gave their lives that that nation might live. It is altogether fitting and proper that we should do this. But in a larger sense we cannot dedicate, we cannot consecrate, we cannot hallow this ground. The brave men, living and dead, who struggled here, have consecrated it, far above our poor power to add or detract. The world will little note, nor long remember, what we say here, but it can never forget what they did here. It is for us, the living, rather to be dedicated here to the unfinished work which they who fought here have thus far so nobly advanced. It is rather for us to be here dedicated to the great task remaining before us, that from these honored dead we take increased devotion to that cause for which they gave the last full measure of devotion; that we here highly resolve that these dead shall not have died in vain; that this nation, under God, shall have a new birth of freedom; and that government of the people, by the people, for the people, shall not perish from the earth.

LINCOLN IS RE-ELECTED PRESIDENT

The war was still unfinished when Lincoln's first term as President came to an end. He was re-elected for a second term, and was inaugurated in March, 1865.

Lincoln could then foresee the end of the war, and in his second inaugural address he showed the people how curious and sad it was that both the North and the South should be reading the same Bible and praying to the same God, each calling upon Him for aid against the other. "Fondly do we hope, fervently do we pray," he said, "that this mighty scourge of war may speedily pass away." But he could see no other way than to keep on fighting until the question was decided between union and no union, between freedom and slavery.

With what mixed feelings Lincoln must have accepted a second term as President of our country. He, more than any other man, could foresee the difficulties which lay ahead in welding the North and South once more into a united nation. In his heart were only sympathy and understanding for both. Boundless patience and tactful guidance would be needed. The undertaking must have seemed enormous to a man worn with four years of carrying the greatest possible burdens. The spirit in which he accepted the task that lay ahead is clearly shown in these words from his second inaugural speech, "With malice towards none, with charity for all."

FROM ABRAHAM LINCOLN'S SECOND INAUGURAL ADDRESS

March, 1865

With malice towards none, with charity for all, with firmness in the right, as God gives us to see the right, let us strive on to finish the work we are in, to bind up the nation's wounds, to care for him who shall have borne the battle, and for his widow and orphans; to do all which may achieve and cherish a just and a lasting peace among ourselves and with all nations.

THE QUESTION OF SLAVERY IS SETTLED

The fall of Richmond in April, 1865, marked the end of the War between the States. Lee's army was trapped between Grant's Union forces on the north and Sheridan's on the south. On April 9, 1865, Lee surrendered. Five days later, Lincoln was dead, the victim of an assassin's bullet.

The war had lasted four years. The Thirteenth Amendment, which prohibited slavery within the United States and in any territory controlled by it, was made a part of the Constitution in December, 1865.

Once more the nation was united. Lincoln's words, "With malice towards none, with charity for all," are reflected in the poem "The Blue and the Gray," a tribute to the men of both sides who fell in the struggle.

THE BLUE AND THE GRAY

FRANCIS M. FINCH

By the flow of the inland river,
   Whence the fleets of iron have fled,
Where the blades of the grave-grass quiver,
   Asleep are the ranks of the dead,—
     Under the sod and the dew;
      Waiting the judgment day;
     Under the one, the Blue;
      Under the other, the Gray.

These in the robings of glory,
  Those in the gloom of defeat;
All with the battle-blood gory,
  In the dusk of eternity meet,—
    Under the sod and the dew;
      Waiting the judgment day;
    Under the laurel, the Blue;
      Under the willow, the Gray.

From the silence of sorrowful hours
  The desolate mourners go,
Lovingly laden with flowers,
  Alike for the friend and the foe;
    Under the sod and the dew;
      Waiting the judgment day;
    Under the roses, the Blue;
      Under the lilies, the Gray.

So, with an equal splendor,
  The morning sun-rays fall,
With a touch impartially tender,
  On the blossoms blooming for all,—
    Under the sod and the dew;
      Waiting the judgment day;
    Broidered with gold, the Blue;
      Mellowed with gold, the Gray.

So, when the summer calleth
  On forest, and field of grain,

With an equal murmur falleth
  The cooling drip of the rain;
    Under the sod and the dew;
      Waiting the judgment day;
    Wet with the rain, the Blue;
      Wet with the rain, the Gray.

Sadly, but not with upbraiding,
  The generous deed was done;
In the storm of the years now fading
  No braver battle was won;
    Under the sod and the dew;
      Waiting the judgment day;
    Under the blossoms, the Blue;
      Under the garlands, the Gray.

No more shall the war cry sever,
  Or the winding rivers be red;
They banish our anger forever
  When they laurel the graves of our dead.
    Under the sod and the dew;
      Waiting the judgment day;
    Love and tears for the Blue;
      Tears and love for the Gray.

"YOU WOULDN'T KNOW ABOUT MY SON?"

Lincoln's mother, Nancy Hanks, died when Abe was nine years old. She left him a lanky, awkward boy, living in a rough log cabin in the wilds of Indiana. How she hoped life would not be too hard for him, though there was little promise that much would come his way.

The poet Rosemary Benét has pictured Lincoln's mother as still anxious about her boy, still hoping that he "got on."

NANCY HANKS

ROSEMARY BENÉT

If Nancy Hanks
    Came back as a ghost,
Seeking news
    Of what she loved most,
She'd ask first
    "Where's my son?
What's happened to Abe?
    What's he done?

"Poor little Abe,
    Left all alone,
Except for Tom
    Who's a rolling stone;

He was only nine
  The year I died.
I remember still
  How hard he cried.

"Scraping along
  In a little shack,
With hardly a shirt
  To cover his back,
And a prairie wind
  To blow him down,
Or pinching times
  If he went to town.

"You wouldn't know
  About my son?
Did he grow tall?
  Did he have fun?
Did he learn to read?
  Did he get to town?
Do you know his name?
  Did he get on?"

LIBERTY ENLIGHTENING THE WORLD

On a little island in New York harbor, looking out towards Europe, stands the highest statue in the world. It is 151 feet high and, together with its foundation and pedestal, towers 305 feet above the water. At its top is a glass torch that can hold twelve people, and forty persons can stand inside its head.

But it is not the bigness of the Statue of Liberty that makes Americans proud of it. It is what that statue means. France gave it to us. The French people, after a hundred years of suffering, struggle, and bloodshed, and a terrible war with Prussia, had become a republic. They remembered the great sympathy of their forefathers for us when we were fighting for our freedom, and they knew that the United States would soon celebrate the hundredth birthday of American independence. They wanted to show our country that the two nations were brothers, united by love of liberty.

A noted French sculptor, Frederic Auguste Bartholdi, designed and made the Statue of Liberty. French people, rich and poor alike, contributed the $250,000 needed to make it. Americans subscribed $350,000 for the pedestal and the cost of erecting the statue in New York.

In 1886 the statue of "Liberty Enlightening the World" was unveiled at a memorable ceremony in

THE STATUE OF LIBERTY

To immigrants entering New York harbor this noble statue holds forth the promise of "life, liberty, and the pursuit of happiness." It is an inspiration to all Americans. The statue was presented to us by France on the one hundredth anniversary of our independence.

which warships fired salutes and statesmen of both
countries made speeches. The statue is the figure of
a woman bearing in her left hand a tablet carrying
the inscription "July 4, 1776," and with the other
hand holding aloft a torch.

The Statue of Liberty is eagerly watched for by
home-coming American travelers and by people from
less fortunate countries who have crossed the Atlantic
to find freedom and self-government in the New
World.

WILLIAM McKINLEY

During McKinley's first term as President, the United States acquired the Hawaiian Islands, the Philippines, and the islands of Puerto Rico, Guam, and Tutuila. McKinley was assassinated in 1901, during his second term in office.

OUR COUNTRY THE FOE OF OPPRESSION

THE LITTLE WAR THAT FREED CUBA

For centuries Cuba was a Spanish possession. The Spanish governors oppressed the people, taxing them heavily and allowing them no part in their government. There were frequent rebellions, one of the most serious of them occurring in 1895. To crush this rebellion, the Spanish governor of the island had the people driven into concentration camps, where many of them died from starvation and disease.

For a long time the people of the United States had looked with disfavor on the Spanish treatment of the Cubans. Furthermore, many Americans had invested money in sugar plantations on the island and these were being ruined in the struggles. Our country sent repeated protests to Spain, and an unfriendly feeling existed between the two countries.

Then, on February 15, 1898, while the American battleship *Maine* was on a friendly visit to Cuba, it was blown up in the harbor of Havana. More than 260 American sailors lost their lives in the explosion.

From all parts of our country came the demand for war with Spain. But President McKinley waited for the report of a committee which was appointed to investigate the cause of the explosion. When they reported that the explosion had come from outside the ship, the President laid the facts before Congress, which immediately declared war on Spain.

Within three months, the American navy had destroyed the Spanish fleets at Cuba and in the Philippine Islands, also owned by Spain; and Spain asked for peace. By the terms of the treaty, Spain gave up Cuba and turned over to the United States the islands of Puerto Rico, the Philippines, and Guam in return for a payment of $20,000,000. Cuba set up a republican government under United States protection, and in 1902 was granted her complete independence.

PRESIDENT McKINLEY'S WAR MESSAGE

FROM THE MESSAGE OF PRESIDENT WILLIAM McKINLEY TO THE HOUSE OF REPRESENTATIVES, APRIL 11, 1898.

It becomes my duty now to address you with regard to the grave crisis that has arisen in the relations of the United States to Spain by reason of the warfare that for more than three years has raged in the neighboring island of Cuba.

Since the present revolution began in 1895 this country has seen the fertile domain at our threshold ravaged by fire and sword in the course of a struggle unequalled in the history of the island and rarely paralleled as to the numbers of combatants and the bitterness of the contest by any revolution of modern times where a dependent people striving to be free have been opposed by the power of the sovereign state.

THE UNITED STATES BATTLESHIP *MAINE*

On February 15, 1898, the *Maine* was lying peacefully in Havana harbor, Cuba.   Suddenly a violent explosion shook the ship and she plunged to the bottom, carrying with her more than 260 officers and men.   Blame for the incident was laid to Spanish agents, and the United States immediately went to war with Spain.

As I said in my message of last December, it was not civilized warfare; it was extermination.   The only peace it could beget was that of the wilderness and the grave.

Forcible intervention is justifiable:

First.   In the cause of humanity and to put an end to the barbarities, bloodshed, starvation, and horrible miseries now existing there.

It is no answer to say that this is all in another

country, belonging to another nation and is therefore none of our business. It is specially our duty for it is right at our door.

Second. We owe it to our citizens in Cuba to afford them that protection for life and property which no government there can or will afford.

Third. The right to intervene may be justified by the very serious injury to the commerce, trade, and business of our people and by the wanton destruction of property and devastation of the island.

Fourth. The present condition of affairs in Cuba is a constant menace to our peace. I have already sent to Congress the report of the naval court of inquiry on the destruction of the battleship *Maine* in the harbor of Havana during the night of the fifteenth of February. The destruction of that noble vessel has filled the national heart with horror. Two hundred and fifty-eight brave sailors and marines and two officers of our navy reposing in the fancied security of a friendly harbor, have been hurled to death.

The issue is now with Congress. It is a solemn responsibility. I have exhausted every effort to relieve the intolerable condition of affairs which is at our doors. Prepared to execute every obligation imposed upon me by the Constitution and the law, I await your action.

SENATOR LODGE'S SPEECH ON WAR WITH SPAIN

Delivered in the United States Senate,
April 13, 1898.

If war must be—I hope and pray that it may yet be avoided—no nation ever went to war on higher grounds or from nobler or more disinterested motives. War is here, if it is here, by the act of Spain.   We have grasped no man's territory.   We have taken no man's property.   We have invaded no man's rights. We do not ask their lands.   We do not ask their money.   We ask peace in that unhappy island—peace and freedom, not for ourselves, but for others.

It is an unselfish, a pure, a noble demand, and if war does come, then, Mr. President, we do not fear to meet it.   We will meet it so that the curse of Spain shall never rest again on any part of the Western Hemisphere.   We do not want war: we would do anything in honor to avoid it; but if it must come, it will be a war that will prevent Spain from ever bringing misery, death, and ruin to Cuba, and agitation, unhappiness, loss, and war to the United States.

And now, Mr. President, what of the *Maine?* I am so sentimental, I am so merely human, that that ship is nearer my heart than anything else. Suppose she had gone down to her death in an English harbor, blown up as she was, carrying her

Brown Brothers, N. Y.

HENRY CABOT LODGE

Henry Cabot Lodge was Senator from Massachusetts for thirty-one years. He was one of our foremost historians and wrote many books, including stories of the lives of Washington, Hamilton, and Webster, and a history of the United States.

men with her; what do you think would have been the voice of England—the land of Nelson? I believe if it had happened in an English port England would have said, in a great and generous spirit, "We regard this with horror, we believe that it must have been an accident, but it happened in our harbor under our flag. If you think otherwise name the reparation that you want."

Such, Mr. President, I believe, would have been the reply of England; such I believe would have been our reply or that of any of the great powers.

Look now at Spain. She has done nothing but slander officers and sailors of the *Maine*, dead and living. Her ambassador to Rome said but a week ago to all Europe in a published interview, that that ship went down because her captain neglected her and was not on board. Notorious as the sinking of the ship is, the fact that Captain Sigsbee was there and was the last man to leave, is equally well known, and yet the Spanish ambassador to Rome tells that lying story to the world.

They rejoiced in Havana and they explained the explosion by throwing it upon our officers, slandering their character and denying their words. I have no more doubt about it than that I am now standing in the Senate of the United States, that that ship was blown up by a government mine.

Others may reason from the facts as they please. To me they bear but one interpretation, and that is that the *Maine* went to her death by Spanish treachery in the harbor of Havana and Spaniards exulted and feasted when the black deed was done.

It may be urged that we should negotiate and arbitrate, but whenever I think of that solution there comes to my mind the lines of Lowell, written at another period, a very dark time in this country:

> Ef I turn mad dogs loose, John,
>   On your front parlor stairs,
> Would it jest meet your views, John,
>   To wait an' sue their heirs?

At the close of the Civil War the great war governor of Massachusetts found his practice scattered, his small accumulations and savings gone, because he had given his time, as, indeed, he gave his life to the service of the State and the country. It was known how much he had suffered in his practice and his purse and there was a story circulated in the papers that his friends intended to make him collector of the port, the most highly paid office in the State of Massachusetts.

The day that item of news appeared, a friend of Governor Andrew met him and said to him, "Well, Governor, are you going to take the collectorship?" He paused a moment, then looked up suddenly and said, "I have stood for four years as high priest between the horns of the altar; I have poured out upon it the best blood of Massachusetts; I cannot take money for that."

Mr. President, we cannot take money for the dead

men of the *Maine*. There is only one reparation. There is only one monument to raise over that grave, and that is free Cuba and peace in that island. That is a worthy monument, worthy of men who died under the flag they loved, died "in the line of duty."

I care but little what form of words we adopt. I am ready to yield my opinions to those about me in Congress. Still more ready am I to defer to the wishes of the Executive, who stands, and must stand, at our head; but I want now to arm that Executive with powers which shall enable him, in the good providence of God, to bring peace to Cuba and exact justice for the *Maine*.

THE UNITED STATES NOT A WARLIKE NATION

ROBERT CAMERON ROGERS

We are not a warlike nation; here of old our fathers
    settled,
Seeking scope for their opinions, in the log house
    and the hut;
Seeking elbow room and freedom, sober men and
    quiet mettled,
Almost too religious, maybe, peaceful-minded people;
    but—

Since they wished to farm the meadows, wished to
    go to church on Sunday,

And the redskin would annoy them with his lust for
   human hair,
From far Georgia to the south'ard, to the misty
   shore of Fundy,
Flintlocks kept the plough a-going, bullets helped to
   speed the prayer.

We are not a warlike nation; though the blood we
   brought was ruddy,
We preferred its cherry runnels in the veins kept
   tightly shut.
We had thews for farm and fishnet; we had brains
   to scheme and study;
Brawn and brain for peace and quiet,—that was all
   we wanted; but—

Ask the fields of sleepy Concord, ask old wrecked
   Ticonderoga,
Of the cost of unjust taxes and old bottles for new
   wine!
Something more than glass was broken on the heights
   of Saratoga,
And the tax was paid at Yorktown by the stiff old
   buff-blue line.

We are not a warlike nation; patterned, rather, for
   keen trading;
Some will say the style is English, that from them
   we get the cut;

East and west our ships went speeding, decks awash
    from heavy lading;
Bowsprits poked in every harbor, never seeking
    quarrels; but—

When our rich Levant trade came, and Tripoli
    claimed tribute from it,—
Tribute paid by other navies trading down the mid-
    land sea,—
We, the least and last of nations, blew her gunboats
    to Mahomet,
Blew the faithful to their houris, made the straits
    forever free.

We are not a warlike nation; we had states to form
    and settle,
We had stuffs to manufacture, till our markets felt
    the glut;
We were busy getting headway, busy panning out
    the metal
From the human dust that reached us from the old-
    world digging; but—

We could slow up for a moment, just to show our
    elder brother
That the bird we put our faith in was not stuffed
    upon his perch;
And we told him through the cannon, in the sea
    fights' reek and smother,
We had searched the Scripture duly, but had found
    no "right to search."

We are not a warlike nation; peace sometimes keeps
　　men's souls sleeping;
Some of us still sought our harvests in the old barbaric
　　rut
Worn by captive feet, till, one day, party feeling
　　upward leaping,
Broke into a flame and blazed on all the startled
　　nations; but—

When the smoke from red fields lifted, when the
　　armies were disbanded,—
Better armies, all the world knows, never cartridge
　　bit or rammed,—
Proud of their own deeds, and proud, too, of the men
　　who, lighter handed,
Fought them long and ofttimes whipped them,
　　slavery was dead and damned.

We are not a warlike nation; we love life far more
　　than dying;
We have little time for swagger and the military
　　strut;
Let old Europe pay big armies; we have better fish
　　for frying,
We have nobler tools for manhood than the sword
　　and rifle; but—

Since we are a Christian nation, and the blood our
　　veins are filled with—

Anglo-Saxon, Celtic, Teuton—will not keep forever
    cool,
When we see weak women starving, helpless, ill-
    starred children killed with
Filthy water, air empoisoned, just to eke out Spanish
    rule;

Since we find that Cuba's Cuban, and the Spaniard
    but a tenant
Who defiles the house he lives in, then our duty
    stands out plain;
We are masters in these waters, at the mainmast
    flies our pennant,
End this hell on earth, or, hark ye, eastward lies the
    path to Spain.

DEWEY'S FLAGSHIP, THE *OLYMPIA*

In the battle between the American and Spanish fleets at Manila, in the Philippines, every Spanish ship was sunk and the Americans lost not a single man. Leading the American squadron, on the flagship *Olympia*, was Commodore George Dewey.

When news of the battle of Manila Bay reached the United States, Dewey was hailed as a hero, and was given the rank of Rear Admiral. Later he was appointed Admiral of the Navy. The *Olympia*, his flagship, became one of the hero-ships of our navy, thought of in the same way as the *Bon Homme Richard*, the *Constitution*, and the *Monitor*.

Forty years later, Dewey's flagship, an outworn and obsolete vessel, was condemned to be cut up and sold as scrap metal. To many patriotic lovers of the navy, this seemed an unhappy end for so famous a ship. Some suggested that she be made a floating naval museum, as the *Constitution*—"*Old Ironsides*"—had been. Others had different ideas. An anonymous writer penned the following poem and sent it to the Navy Department, hoping that it might help to save the *Olympia* from "the hacksaw's bite, the blow torch' flaming breath." Unfortunately, it did not. The staunch old *Olympia* was cut up and sold as scrap metal.

THE *OLYMPIA* SPEAKS

AUTHOR UNKNOWN

They wonder, now, about my fate
    Since I'm not fit for sea.
They ask opinions right and left
    But no one questions me.

Oh, spare me from the hack-saw's bite,
    The blow-torch' flaming breath.
A coward ship that never fought
    Would merit such a death.

Nor let me, like *Old Ironsides*,
    Lie waiting to decay,
While younger, stronger fighting craft
    Sail by me down the bay.

And save me from the bitter fate
    That claimed the *Texas* old—
A target sunk by sister craft
    While cannon thunder rolled.

I never earned that traitor death—
    That rending hail of shot.
Too bad to let our cannon do
    What Spanish guns could not!

But let me, like the murdered *Maine,*
  Be taken far from shore
And sunk to rest beneath the wave,
  At peace forevermore.

And as my flag, still flying free,
  Shall sink beneath the wave,
Let taps be played, as when they lay
  A hero in his grave.

THE MODERN PERIOD

WHY WE ENTERED THE FIRST WORLD WAR

There were many underlying causes of the World War of 1914-1918. Germany had started a bitter rivalry with Great Britain for the control of the world's commerce. This led to a naval race, with each nation striving to build a larger warfleet than the other. Germany and France had twice come to the point of blows over colonial claims in Africa. Germany and Russia both had designs on Constantinople, a Turkish city which controlled the straits between Europe and Asia. All of these situations were dangerous. Worst of all was the existence of two great alliances: the Triple Alliance, consisting of Germany, Austria-Hungary, and Italy; and the Triple Entente, consisting of Great Britain, France, and Russia.

The act which was used as an excuse for starting the war was the assassination of Archduke Francis Ferdinand, of Austria, by a citizen of Serbia. Austria promptly made some unreasonable demands upon the Serbian government and followed with a declaration of war. Russia came to Serbia's defense, and Germany sided with Austria. France stood by her ally, Russia, and went to war against Germany. In order to invade France by the easiest route, Germany sent her troops through the small, neutral country of Belgium. This brought Great Britain into the war, for the British government had signed a treaty guaranteeing Belgium's neutrality. British statesmen also felt that it would be dangerous for their country if German troops were allowed to occupy Belgium.

The war started well for Germany. German troops swept through Belgium and northern France, driving the Belgian, French, and British troops before them. It was only when the river Marne was reached, a few miles from Paris, that France and her allies were able to stop the advance. There, in the Battle of the Marne, the German troops were halted and hurled back. Both sides at once dug trenches and prepared for a long fight. This line of battle, called the western front, remained almost unchanged for more than two years.

Meanwhile, the Russians had invaded both Germany and Austria. At first they were successful, but they later suffered a series of defeats and were driven out of both countries and forced far back into their own territory.

In the North Sea, the British won a naval victory over the Germans in the battle of Jutland. The German ships retired to their harbors, and the mighty British fleet proceeded to blockade Germany in an attempt to win the war by starvation. The Germans, for their part, tried to starve the British by sending out submarines to attack all merchant ships approaching the British Isles with supplies.

As the war progressed, other nations entered it. Japan came into the war to help Great Britain and France and to gain for herself certain German islands in the Pacific. Late in 1914 Turkey joined the Central Powers, as Germany and Austria-Hungary were called. Later, Bulgaria also joined the same side. In spite of being a member of the Triple Alliance, Italy broke with Germany and Austria-Hungary and came into the war on the side of the Allies. Rumania also joined the Allies.

At first the United States tried to remain neutral. President Wilson warned all Americans to be "neutral in thought as well as deed." But it was hard to be neutral. The war was exciting, and almost at once Americans found themselves taking sides. Although Americans whose families had recently come from Germany or France or Great Britain naturally sided with their mother countries, more and more the people of our country, regardless of their original nationalities, found themselves siding with the Allies. Germany's ruthless invasion of Belgium, without excuse, offended our ideal of fair play. The gallant resistance of the Belgians, and of the French at the Marne, aroused admiration in this country.

Then German submarines began sinking American ships, and German spies tried to destroy American factories supplying munitions to the Allies. In spite of repeated protests, the submarines and the spies continued their activities. The situation could no longer be tolerated. On April 2, 1917, President Wilson spoke before Congress, urging that the United States join the Allies. Four days later, we declared war on Germany.

WOODROW WILSON

During the early years of the first World War, President Wilson strove to keep our country neutral. When Germany started unrestricted submarine warfare in 1917, the President asked Congress to declare war.

PRESIDENT WILSON'S WAR MESSAGE

Delivered April 2, 1917

GENTLEMEN OF CONGRESS:

I have called the Congress into extraordinary session because there are serious, very serious, choices of policy to be made and made immediately, which it was neither right nor constitutionally permissible that I should assume the responsibility of making.

On the third of February last I officially laid before you the extraordinary announcement of the Imperial German Government that on and after the first day of February it was its purpose to put aside all restraints of law or of humanity and use its submarines to sink every vessel that sought to approach either the ports of Great Britain and Ireland, or the western coasts of Europe, or any of the ports controlled by the enemies of Germany within the Mediterranean. That had seemed to be the object of the German submarine warfare earlier in the war, but since April of last year the Imperial Government had somewhat restrained the commanders of its undersea craft in conformity with its promise then given to us that passenger-boats should not be sunk and that due warning would be given to all other vessels which its submarines might seek to destroy when no resistance was offered or escape attempted, and care taken that their crews were given at least a fair chance to save their lives in their open boats. The precautions taken were meager and haphazard enough, as was proved in distressing instance after instance in the progress of the cruel and unmanly business, but a certain degree of restraint was observed.

GERMANY'S RUTHLESS POLICY

The new policy has swept every restriction aside. Vessels of every kind, whatever their flag, their character, their cargo, their destination, their errand, have been ruthlessly sent to the bottom without warning, and without thought of help or mercy for those on board, the vessels of friendly neutrals along with those of belligerents. Even hospital-ships and ships carrying relief to the sorely bereaved and stricken people of Belgium, though the latter were provided with safe conduct through the prescribed areas by the German Government itself and were distinguished by unmistakable marks of identity, have been sunk with the same reckless lack of compassion or of principle.

I was for a little while unable to believe that such things would, in fact, be done by any government that had hitherto subscribed to the humane practices of civilized nations. International law had its origin in the attempt to set up some law which would be respected and observed upon the seas where no nation had right of dominion, and where lay the free highways of the world. By painful stage after stage has that law been built up, with meager enough results indeed, after all was accomplished that could be accomplished, but always with a clear view, at least, of what the heart and conscience of mankind demanded.

This minimum of right the German Government has swept aside under the plea of retaliation and necessity and because it had no weapons which it could use at sea except those which it is impossible to employ as it is employing them without throwing to the winds all scruples of humanity or of respect for the understandings that were supposed to underlie the intercourse of the world. I am not now thinking of the loss of property involved, immense and serious as that is, but only of the wanton and wholesale destruction of the lives of non-combatants, men, women, and children, engaged in pursuits which have always, even in the darkest periods of modern history, been deemed innocent and legitimate. Property can be paid for; the lives of peaceful and innocent people cannot be.

German Warfare against Mankind

The present German submarine warfare against commerce is a warfare against mankind.

It is a war against all nations. American ships have been sunk, American lives taken, in ways which it has stirred us very deeply to learn of, but the ships and people of other neutral and friendly nations have been sunk and overwhelmed in the waters in the same way. There has been no discrimination. The challenge is to all mankind. Each nation must decide for itself how it will meet it. The choice we make for ourselves must be made with a moderation of counsel and a temperateness of judgment befitting our character and our motives as a nation. We must put excited feeling away. Our motive will not be revenge or the victorious assertion of the physical might of the nation, but only the vindication of right, of human right, of which we are only a single champion.

When I addressed the Congress on the twenty-sixth of February last I thought that it would suffice to assert our neutral rights with arms, our right to use the seas against unlawful interference, our right to keep our people safe against unlawful violence. But armed neutrality, it now appears, is impracticable. Because submarines are in effect outlaws when used as the German submarines have been used against merchant shipping, it is impossible to defend ships against their attacks as the law of nations has assumed that merchantmen would defend themselves against privateers or cruisers, visible craft giving chase upon the open sea.

It is common prudence, in such circumstances, grim necessity indeed, to endeavor to destroy them before they have shown their own intention. They must be dealt with upon sight, if dealt with at all. The German Government denies the right of neutrals to use arms at all within the areas of the sea which it has proscribed, even in the defense of rights which no modern publicist has ever before questioned their right to defend.

The intimation is conveyed that the armed guards which we have placed on our merchant ships will be treated as beyond the pale of law and subject to be dealt with as pirates would be.

Armed neutrality is ineffectual cnough at best; in such circumstances and in the face of such pretensions it is worse than ineffectual; it is likely only to produce what it was meant to prevent; it is practically certain to draw us into the war without either the rights or the effectiveness of belligerents.

There is one choice we cannot make, we are incapable of making: we will not choose the path of submission and suffer the most sacred rights of our nation and our people to be ignored or violated. The wrongs against which we now array ourselves are no common wrongs; they cut to the very roots of human life.

War Thrust Upon Us

With a profound sense of the solemn and even tragical character of the step I am taking and of the grave responsibilities which it involves, but in unhesitating obedience to what I deem my constitutional duty, I advise that the Congress declare the recent course of the Imperial German Government to be in fact nothing less than war against the government and people of the United States; that it formally accept the status of belligerent which has thus been thrust upon it; and that it take immediate steps not only to put the country in a more thorough state of defense, but also to exert all its power and employ all its resources to bring the government of the German Empire to terms and end the war.

What This Means

What this will involve is clear. It will involve the utmost practicable co-operation in counsel and action with the governments now at war with Germany, and, as incident to that, the extension to those governments of the most liberal financial credits in order that our resources may, so far as possible, be added to theirs. It will involve the organization and mobilization of all the material resources of the country to supply the materials of war and serve the incidental needs of the nation in the most abundant, and yet the most economical and efficient way possible.

It will involve the immediate full equipment of the navy in all respects, but particularly in supplying it with the best means of dealing with the enemy's submarines. It will involve the immediate addition to the armed forces of the United States already provided for by law in case of war, at least 500,000 men, who should, in my opinion, be chosen upon the principle of universal liability to service, and also the authorization of subsequent additional increments of equal force so soon as they may be needed and can be handled in training.

It will involve also, of course, the granting of adequate credits to the Government, sustained, I hope, so far as they can equitably be sustained by the present generation, by well conceived taxation. I say sustained so far as may be equitable by taxation because it seems to me that it would be most unwise to base the credits which will now be necessary entirely on money borrowed. It is our duty, I most respectfully urge, to protect our people so far as we may against the very serious hardships and evils which would be likely to arise out of the inflation which would be produced by vast loans.

In carrying out the measures by which these things are to be accomplished, we should keep constantly in mind the wisdom of interfering as little as possible in our own preparation and in the equipment of our own military forces with the duty—for it will be a very practical duty—of supplying the nations already at war with Germany with the materials which they can obtain only from us or by our assistance. They are in the field and we should help them in every way to be effective there.

I shall take the liberty of suggesting, through the several executive departments of the Government, for the consideration of your committees, measures for the accomplishment of the several objects I have mentioned. I hope that it will be your pleasure to deal with them as having been framed after very careful thought by the branch of the Government upon which the responsibility of conducting the war and safeguarding the nation will most directly fall.

Our Motives and Objects

While we do these things, these deeply momentous things, let us be very clear and make very clear to all the world what our motives and our objects are. My own thought has not been driven from its habitual and normal course by the unhappy events of the last two months, and I do not believe that the thought of the nation has been altered or clouded by them.

I have exactly the same things in mind now that I had in mind when I addressed the Senate on the twenty-second of January last; the same that I had in mind when I addressed the Congress on the third of February and on the twenty-sixth of February. Our object now, as then, is to vindicate the principles of peace and justice in the life of the world as against selfish and autocratic power, and to set up amongst the really free and self-governed peoples of the world such a concert of purpose and of action as will henceforth insure the observance of those principles.

Neutrality is no longer feasible or desirable where the peace of the world is involved and the freedom of its peoples, and the menace to that peace and freedom lies in the existence of autocratic governments backed by organized force which is controlled wholly by their will, not by the will of their people. We have seen the last of neutrality in such circumstances.

We are at the beginning of an age in which it will be insisted that the same standards of conduct and of responsibility for wrong done shall be observed among nations and their governments that are observed among the individual citizens of civilized states.

We have no quarrel with the German people. We have no feeling towards them but one of sympathy and friendship. It was not upon their impulse that their Government acted in entering this war. It was not with their previous knowledge or approval.

It was a war determined upon as wars used to be determined upon in the old, unhappy days when peoples were nowhere consulted by their rulers and wars were provoked and waged in the interests of dynasties or of little groups of ambitious men who were accustomed to use their fellow men as pawns and tools.

Self-governed nations do not fill their neighbor states with spies or set the course of intrigue to bring about some critical posture of affairs which will give them an opportunity to strike and make conquest. Such designs can be successfully worked out only under cover and where no one has the right to ask questions.

Cunningly contrived plans of deception or aggression, carried, it may be, from generation to generation, can be worked out and kept from the light only within the privacy of courts or behind the carefully guarded confidences of a narrow and privileged class. They are happily impossible where public opinion commands and insists upon full information concerning all the nation's affairs.

PEACE THROUGH FREE PEOPLES

A steadfast concert for peace can never be maintained except by a partnership of democratic nations. No autocratic government could be trusted to keep faith within it or observe its covenants.

It must be a league of honor, a partnership of opinion. Intrigue would eat its vitals away; the plottings of inner circles who could plan what they would and render account to no one would be a corruption seated at its very heart. Only free peoples can hold their purpose and their honor steady to a common end and prefer the interests of mankind to any narrow interest of their own. . . .

One of the things that has served to convince us that the Prussian autocracy was not and could never be our friend is that from the very outset of the present war it has filled our unsuspecting communities, and even our offices of government, with spies, and set criminal intrigues everywhere afoot against our national unity of counsel, our peace within and without, our industries and our commerce.

Indeed, it is now evident that its spies were here even before the war began; and it is, unhappily, not a matter of conjecture but a fact proved in our courts of justice that the intrigues which have more than once come perilously near to disturbing the peace and dislocating the industries of the country have been carried on at the instigation, with the support, and even under the personal direction of official agents of the Imperial German Government accredited to the Government of the United States.

Even in checking these things and trying to extirpate them we have sought to put the most generous interpretation possible upon them, because we knew that their source lay, not in any hostile feeling or purpose of the German people towards us (who were, no doubt, as ignorant of them as we ourselves were), but only in the selfish designs of a Government that did what it pleased and told its people nothing. But they have played their part in serving to convince us at last that that Government entertains no real friendship for us and means to act against our peace and security at its convenience.

That it means to stir up enemies against us at our very doors the intercepted note to the German Minister at Mexico City is eloquent evidence.

ACCEPTING THE CHALLENGE

We are accepting this challenge of hostile purpose because we know that in such a government, following such methods we can never have a friend; and that in the presence of its organized power, always lying in wait to accomplish we know not what purpose, there can be no assured security for the democratic governments of the world.

We are now about to accept gage of battle with this natural foe to liberty, and shall, if necessary, spend the whole force of the nation to check and nullify its pretensions and its power. We are glad, now that we see the facts with no veil of false pretense about them, to fight thus for the ultimate peace of the world and for the liberation of its peoples, the German people included; for the rights of nations, great and small, and the privilege of men everywhere to choose their way of life and of obedience. The world must be made safe for democracy; its peace must be planted upon tested foundations of political liberty.

We have no selfish ends to serve. We desire no conquest, no dominion. We seek no indemnities for ourselves, no material compensation for the sacrifices we shall freely make. We are but one of the champions of the rights of mankind. We shall be satisfied when those rights have been made as secure as the faith and the freedom of the nations can make them.

Just because we fight without rancor and without selfish object, seeking nothing for ourselves but what we shall wish to share with all free peoples, we shall, I feel confident, conduct our operations as belligerents without passion and ourselves observe with proud punctilio the principles of right and of fair play we profess to be fighting for.

I have said nothing of the governments allied with the Imperial Government of Germany because they have not made war upon us or challenged us to defend our right and our honor. The Austro-Hungarian Government has, indeed, avowed its unqualified indorsement and acceptance of the reckless and lawless submarine warfare adopted now without disguise by the Imperial German Government, and it has, therefore, not been possible for this Government to receive Count Tarnowski, the Ambassador recently accredited to this Government by the Imperial and Royal Government of Austria-Hungary; but that Government has not actually engaged in warfare against citizens of the United States on the seas, and I take the liberty, for the present at least, of postponing a discussion of our relations with the authorities at Vienna.

OPPOSITION TO THE GERMAN GOVERNMENT FRIENDSHIP TOWARD THE GERMAN PEOPLE

We enter this war only where we are clearly forced into it because there are no other means of defending our rights.

It will be all the easier for us to conduct ourselves as belligerents in a high spirit of right and fairness because we act without animus, not in enmity towards a people or with the desire to bring any injury or disadvantage upon them, but only in armed opposition to an irresponsible Government which has thrown aside all considerations of humanity and of right and is running amuck.

We are, let me say again, the sincere friends of the German people, and shall desire nothing so much as the early re-establishment of intimate relations of mutual advantage between us, however hard it may be for them, for the time being, to believe that this is spoken from our hearts. We have borne with their present government through all these bitter months because of that friendship—exercising a patience and forbearance which would otherwise have been impossible.

We shall, happily, still have an opportunity to prove that friendship in our daily attitude and actions toward the millions of men and women of German birth and native sympathy who live amongst us and share our life, and we shall be proud to prove it towards all who are in fact loyal to their neighbors and to the Government in the hour of test. They are, most of them, as true and loyal Americans as if they had never known any other fealty or allegiance. They will be prompt to stand with us in rebuking and restraining the few who may be of a different mind and purpose.

If there should be disloyalty, it will be dealt with with a firm hand of stern repression; but, if it lifts its head at all, it will lift it only here and there and without countenance except from a lawless and malignant few.

RIGHT MORE PRECIOUS THAN PEACE

It is a distressing and oppressive duty, gentlemen of the Congress, which I have performed in thus addressing you. There are, it may be, many months of fiery trial and sacrifice ahead of us. It is a fearful thing to lead this great peaceful people into war, into the most terrible and disastrous of all wars, civilization itself seeming to be in the balance. But the right is more precious than peace, and we shall fight for the things which we have always carried nearest our hearts—for democracy, for the right of those who submit to authority to have a voice in their own governments, for the rights and liberties of small nations, for a universal dominion of right by such a concert of free peoples as shall bring peace and safety to all nations and make the world itself at last free.

To such a task we can dedicate our lives and our fortunes, everything that we are and everything that we have, with the pride of those who know that the day has come when America is privileged to spend her blood and her might for the principles that gave her birth and happiness and the peace which she has treasured. God helping her, she can do no other.

PRESIDENT WILSON AND THE PEACE WITH GERMANY

When President Wilson led the United States into the World War against Germany, he did it for the purposes of "making the world safe for Democracy" and of fighting "a war to end all war." With the end of that war and the defeat of Germany, the President deeply hoped that a treaty might be made that would bring about a fair and lasting peace. He had given deep thought to the matter, and had worked out a series of fourteen points which, if carefully observed by the various nations, would, he felt, mean the end of world conflict. Perhaps the most important of these was Point XIV which called for "a League of Nations to secure peace, independence, and territorial security to all countries, large and small." So convinced was President Wilson of the rightness of his plan that he himself went to France to help in the drawing up of the peace treaty.

In the peace conference at Versailles, President Wilson fought hard to have his fourteen points included in the treaty. Though he could not convince the statesmen of Great Britain, France, and the other European nations that all fourteen points were desirable, he did succeed in getting most of these sensible and far-sighted provisions accepted, including the provision for a League of Nations. The Treaty of Versailles was officially signed on June 28, 1919, by the representatives of the various governments, and President Wilson returned home.

One by one, most of the nations of the earth ratified the Treaty of Versailles, bringing what seemed to be a

happy conclusion to the World War. The League of
Nations was created and began to hold meetings and to
attack the outstanding problems which plagued the
world. But the Senate of the United States refused to
ratify the Treaty of Versailles, and the United States did
not join the League of Nations.

In May, 1920, Congress passed a bill providing for a
separate peace with Germany and Austria-Hungary.
President Wilson, bitterly disappointed at the way in
which our country had failed to co-operate in the plans
for world peace, refused to sign the bill. Instead, he
returned it to the House of Representatives with a message stating clearly his reasons for so doing.

President Wilson's veto message reads almost like a
prophecy. Reading between the lines, we can almost
believe that he could foresee the gradual weakening of the
League of Nations, denied the help and co-operation of
the world's richest, greatest country. We can see that
he felt that the world's troubles were not over—world
wars not ended. He appeared to be warning our country
and the world of the rise of other governments bent upon
conquest and the rule of might. His message is not a
happy one, and it makes grim reading.

Although Congress was unable to pass the separate
peace treaty over President Wilson's veto, a similar bill
was passed the next year. President Harding signed it,
and thus officially ended a war which had actually ended
over two years before.

PRESIDENT WILSON'S VETO MESSAGE

To the House of Representatives:

I return herewith, without my signature, House Joint Resolution 327, intended to repeal the Joint Resolution of April 6, 1917, declaring a state of war to exist between the United States and Germany, and the Joint Resolution of December 7, 1917, declaring a state of war to exist between the United States and the Austro-Hungarian Government, and to declare a state of peace. I have not felt at liberty to sign this resolution because I cannot bring myself to become party to an action which would place ineffaceable stain upon the gallantry and honor of the United States.

The resolution seeks to establish peace with the German Empire without exacting from the German Government any action by way of setting right the infinite wrongs which it did to the peoples whom it attacked and whom we professed it our purpose to assist when we entered the war. Have we sacrificed the lives of more than one hundred thousand Americans and ruined the lives of thousands of others and brought upon thousands of American families an unhappiness that can never end for purposes which we do not now care to state or take further steps to attain?

The attainment of these purposes is provided for

in the Treaty of Versailles by terms deemed adequate by the leading statesmen and experts of all the great peoples who were associated in the war against Germany. Do we now not care to join in the effort to secure them?

We entered the war most reluctantly. Our people were profoundly disinclined to take part in a European war, and at last did so only because they became convinced that it could not in truth be regarded as only a European war, but must be regarded as a war in which civilization itself was involved and human rights of every kind as against a belligerent Government. Moreover, when we entered the war we set forth very definitely the purposes for which we entered, partly because we did not wish to be considered as merely taking part in a European contest. This Joint Resolution which I return does not seek to accomplish any of these objects, but in effect makes a complete surrender of the rights of the United States so far as the German Government is concerned.

A treaty of peace was signed at Versailles on the twenty-eighth of June last which did seek to accomplish the objects which we had declared to be in our minds, because all the great Governments and peoples which united against Germany had adopted our declarations of purpose as their own and had in solemn form embodied them in communications to the German Government preliminary to the Armistice of November 11, 1918. But the treaty, as signed at

Versailles, has been rejected by the Senate of the United States, though it has been ratified by Germany. By that rejection and by its methods we have in effect declared that we wish to draw apart and pursue objects and interests of our own, unhampered by any connections of interest or of purpose with other Governments and peoples.

Notwithstanding the fact that upon our entrance into the war we professed to be seeking to assist in the maintenance of common interests, nothing is said in this resolution about the freedom of navigation upon the seas, or the reduction of armaments, or the vindication of the rights of Belgium, or the rectification of wrongs done to France, or the release of the Christian populations of the Ottoman Empire from the intolerable subjugation which they have had for so many generations to endure, or the establishment of an independent Polish State, or the continued maintenance of any kind of understanding among the great powers of the world which would be calculated to prevent in the future such outrages as Germany attempted and in part consummated.

We have now, in effect, declared that we do not care to take any further risks or to assume any further responsibilities with regard to the freedom of nations or the sacredness of international obligations or the safety of independent peoples. Such a peace with Germany—a peace in which none of the essential interests which we had at heart when we entered the war is safeguarded—is, or ought to be, inconceivable, as inconsistent with the dignity of the United States, with the rights and liberties of her citizens, and with the very fundamental conditions of civilization.

I hope that in these statements I have sufficiently set forth the reasons why I have felt it incumbent upon me to withhold my signature.

WOODROW WILSON

The White House, May 27, 1920.

SUSAN B. ANTHONY

To the untiring efforts and high courage of Susan B. Anthony the women of America owe, in large part, the political rights they enjoy today. She felt that there was no true democracy unless women were granted the same rights as men.

WOMEN'S RIGHT TO VOTE

"Taxation without representation is tyranny" was the cry of the early American colonists when England tried to tax them without allowing them a voice in making their own laws. A hundred years later this cry was echoed by an American woman, Susan B. Anthony. The scene was a New York State court-room, and Miss Anthony was on trial. She had voted in the recent presidential election to test whether women, as citizens, had the right to vote. Charged with having broken a law, she calmly faced her accusers.

When the government of the United States was formed, the question of who should vote was left to be decided by the individual states. Only one state—New Jersey—gave this right to women, but it was later withdrawn.

Although women were denied the right to vote and were not expected to take any part in public life, they were obliged to obey the laws; and women who owned property had to pay taxes. Gradually women began to question this state of affairs. They came to feel that as the laws which were passed affected them and their children they should have a voice in making the laws.

The crusade for women's right to vote began on July 19, 1848, at a convention in Seneca Falls, New York. Chief among the leaders of the movement were Elizabeth Cady Stanton, Mrs. Lucretia Mott, Mrs. Martha Wright, and Mrs. Mary Ann McClintock. Susan B. Anthony, then a school teacher in Canajoharie, New York, read an account of the convention in the local newspaper, but the matter did not particularly interest her. Her interest lay in the cause of temperance; she was using her efforts to bring relief to women whose families were being wrecked by drink.

In 1851 Miss Anthony met Elizabeth Cady Stanton, and from then on the two worked together. They soon saw that women's efforts to better conditions could make no headway until women were granted the vote. In 1869 they organized the National Woman Suffrage Association, the purpose of which was to secure an amendment to the Constitution extending suffrage, or the right to vote, to women. In that same year the American Woman Suffrage Association, headed by Henry Ward Beecher, was formed to secure suffrage for women through state amendments.

At first the idea of woman suffrage was greeted by ridicule, and women who spoke for it in public were laughed at or abused.

Then came the presidential election of 1872, and Miss Anthony voted! She was promptly charged with having broken a law, although there was no clause in the Constitution which denied women the right to vote.

While waiting for her trial, Miss Anthony appeared

in fifty post office districts in New York State and delivered a speech on her constitutional rights as she saw them. In her speech she said:

"Friends and Fellow-Citizens: I stand before you under indictment for the alleged crime of having voted illegally at the last presidential election. I shall endeavor to prove to you that, in voting, I not only committed no crime, but simply exercised my 'citizen's right,' guaranteed to me and all United States citizens by the National Constitution beyond the power of any State to deny.

"Our democratic-republican government is based on the idea of the natural right of every individual member thereof to a voice and a vote in making and executing the laws. . . . The Declaration of Independence, the National and State Constitutions, and the organic laws of the Territories, all alike propose to protect the people in the exercise of their God-given rights. Not one of them pretends to bestow rights."

To prove her point Miss Anthony quoted from the Declaration of Independence:

"All men are created equal, and endowed by their Creator with certain inalienable rights. Among these are life, liberty, and the pursuit of happiness. That to secure these, governments are instituted among men, deriving their just powers from the consent of the governed."

Miss Anthony followed this quotation by saying:
"Here is no shadow of government authority over rights, or exclusion of any class from their full and equal enjoyment. Here is pronounced the rights of all men, and 'consequently,' as the Quaker preacher said, 'of all women,' to a voice in the government. And here, in this very first paragraph of the Declaration, is the assertion of the natural right of all to the ballot; for, how can the 'consent of the governed' be given, if the right to vote be denied. . . .

"The Preamble of the Federal Constitution says:

'We, the people of the United States, in order to form a more perfect union, establish justice, insure domestic tranquility, provide for the common defense, promote the general welfare, and secure the blessings of liberty to ourselves and our posterity, do ordain and establish this Constitution for the United States of America.'

"It was 'we, the people,' not 'we, the white male citizens,' nor yet 'we, the male citizens;' but 'we, the whole people,' who formed this Union and we formed it, not to give the blessings of liberty, but to secure them; not to the half of ourselves and the half of our posterity, but to the whole people—women as well as men. It is downright mockery to talk to women of their enjoyment of the blessings of liberty while they are denied the use of the only means of securing them provided by this democratic-republican government—the ballot. . . .

"The Constitution of the State of New York says
that no member of this State shall be disfranchised
or deprived of the rights or privileges secured to any
citizen thereof, unless by the law of the land or the
judgment of his peers. 'The law of the land,' is the
United States Constitution; and there is no provision in that document that can be fairly construed
into a permission to the States to deprive any class of
their citizens of their right to vote. Hence New
York can get no power from that source to disfran-
chise one entire half of her members. . . . Clearly,
then, there is no constitutional ground for the exclusion of women from the ballot box in the State
of New York. No barriers whatever stand today
between women and the exercise of their right to vote
save those of precedent and prejudice. . . ."

The favorable public response to Miss Anthony's
plea was voiced in the New York State newspapers
of the day, the comments of three of which were as
follows:

It is perhaps needless to say that whoever
listens candidly to Susan B. Anthony, no matter
how he previously regarded her and her sentiments, is certain to respect her and them afterwards.—*Geneva Courier.*

If Miss Anthony has converted every man in
Monroe County to her views of the suffrage question, as the district attorney intimates in his
recent efforts to have her case adjourned, it is

pretty good evidence—unless every man in Monroe County is a fool—that the lady has done no wrong. "Her case," remarks the *Auburn Bulletin*, "will probably be carried over to another term, and all she has to do is to canvass and convert another county. A shrewd woman that! Again we say she ought to vote."— *Rochester Democrat and Chronicle*.

When the trial took place, the judge instructed the jury to bring in a verdict of "guilty," and the jury did as they were told to do. Then the judge asked Miss Anthony if she had anything to say. Miss Anthony had plenty to say, but she was interrupted so often that she finally said, "Failing to get this justice . . . I ask not leniency at your hands, but rather the full rigor of the law." The judge sentenced her to pay a fine of $100 and the costs of the trial. She never paid either, for President Grant pardoned her.

Susan B. Anthony's courageous fight won many supporters for the cause of woman suffrage. She died in 1906, but the fight went on. At last the movement was successful, and on August 18, 1920, the Nineteenth Amendment to the Constitution, reading: "The rights of citizens of the United States to vote shall not be denied or abridged by the United States or by any State on account of sex," was adopted.

DEMOCRACY IS AGAIN THREATENED

Following the World War of 1914-1918, our country turned with relief to normal living. For some years Americans devoted themselves to affairs at home. The question of America's responsibilities to the rest of the world, voiced by Woodrow Wilson, were forgotten or put aside.

In Europe, however, certain dictators seized control of their countries' governments and began to think of new and greater conquests. Weakly the other members of the League of Nations attempted to stem the tide of the dictators' ambitions. But most of the countries represented in the League had not yet recovered from the effects of the first World War. Conditions at home were uncertain, and the League shrank from the use of force which might start a new conflict.

In 1931 America was rudely awakened from her self-interest. In that year Japan invaded the Chinese dependency of Manchuria. The League of Nations sent a committee to investigate the affair, and the committee reported that Japan had invaded Manchuria without excuse and should withdraw her forces. The United States also called Japan's attention to the fact that she was violating existing treaties by her action, but Japan refused to stop the invasion.

Then, in 1936, Italy attacked Ethiopia in defiance of the League, and added that African country to her empire. Two years later Germany started to carry out her policy of conquest. It was her avowed intention to bring all of Europe under German domination, and then to extend her power to the rest of the world.

Americans at last realized that their security was threatened; that unless something was done quickly, the democracy which they had so long taken for granted might be swept away by the forces which were destroying democratic government in the Old World.

THE UNITED STATES—THE GOOD NEIGHBOR

The dangers which threatened the United States because of the new World War also threatened her neighbors on the American continents. It seemed sound policy that, like good neighbors, they should get together and discuss their common problems.

The "Good Neighbor" policy of the United States really began when, in 1823, President James Monroe declared that the Western Hemisphere was no longer open to colonization by European powers and that any attempt of those powers to extend their control over any part of the American continents would be an act unfriendly to the United States. Ever since the announcement of the Monroe Doctrine, the United States has stood ready to enforce the principle of "The Americas for Americans," and to protect her neighbors from invasion.

With the passing of the years, it became more and more evident that the American nations should work together. In 1889 the United States invited representatives of the other American nations to meet in Washington, D. C. There was formed the International Union of the American Republics, later to be known as the Pan American Union.

The founding of the Pan American Union has had many worthwhile results. It has led to arbitration of boundary disputes between the different nations and to peaceful settlement of internal troubles. Furthermore, the republics are working together for the improvement

Acme Newspictures, Inc., N. Y.

CORDELL HULL

As Secretary of State during the second World War, Cordell Hull has performed his difficult task with ability and sincerity.

of health conditions, the expansion of communication and transportation lines, the promotion of commerce, and the development of science.

The bonds of friendship between the American republics were further strengthened when Franklin D. Roosevelt, at the time he became President, in 1933, said, "In the field of world policy, I would dedicate this nation to the policy of the Good Neighbor."

The situation created by the second World War again brought representatives of the American nations together. At a meeting held at Havana, Cuba, in July, 1940, Secretary of State Cordell Hull sounded the keynote of the conference. In his speech he made a plea for co-operation in solving the four major problems which confronted the Americas.

THE NEED FOR CO-OPERATION BETWEEN THE AMERICAS

Sections from the text of SECRETARY OF STATE CORDELL HULL's Address to the Foreign Minister's Conference at Havana, Cuba, July 22, 1940.

. . . We are here as representatives of the twenty-one free and independent American republics. We meet when world conditions are perhaps graver than they have ever been before. Our purpose is to devise concrete measures by which a number of pressing problems may be met. Our objective is to safeguard the independence, the peace, and the well-being of the American republics.

American Historical Bureau, N. Y.

PAN AMERICAN BUILDING, WASHINGTON, D. C.

This beautiful building—the symbol of friendship and co-operation among the twenty-one American republics—is a constant reminder that "in union there is strength."

For nearly a year now a new major war has raged with increasing fury, over important areas of the earth. It came as a culmination of a process of deterioration of international conduct and international morality, extending over a period of years, during which forces of ruthless conquest were gathering strength in several parts of the world.

These forces now at work in the world shrink from no means of attaining their ends. In their contempt for all moral and ethical values, they are bent on uprooting the very foundation of orderly relations among nations and on subverting, undermining, and destroying existing social and political institutions within nations.   They have already left in their wake formerly sovereign nations with their independence trampled into dust and millions of proud men and women with their liberties destroyed.

Our American republics had no part in kindling the tragic conflagration which has been sweeping across the world.   On the contrary, severally and jointly, we did everything in our power to stay its outburst. Once the conflict had begun, we did everything we could to limit its spreading.   But it has been increasingly clear that in the vast tragedy which has befallen large proportions of the earth there are dangers to the American nations, as well, which it would be suicidal not to recognize in time and not to prepare to meet fully and decisively.

It has been increasingly clear that our nations must not blind themselves into fatal complacency as so many nations have done to their mortal sorrow, regarding the possibility of attack against them from without or of externally directed attempts from within to undermine their national strength and to subvert their cherished social and political institutions, or both.

Too many nations have only recently paid a tragic price for confidently placing reliance for their safety and security solely upon clearly expressed desire to remain at peace, upon unequivocally proclaimed neutrality, upon scrupulous avoidance of provocation. Conquerors, invaders, and destroyers ignore or brush aside reasons such as these.

Looming ominously on our horizon is the danger that attempts may be made to employ against our nations, too, the same means of subordinating their destinies to control and dictation from abroad that have already been notoriously employed elsewhere against numerous other countries. We must recognize the serious possibility that no effort or method may be spared to achieve, with respect to some of us, economic domination and political penetration, and to sow, among our nations, the seeds of suspicion, dissension, and discord—the frequent prelude to even more menacing action.

Lest our nations, too, suffer the fate that has already befallen so many peace-loving and peace-seeking nations, wisdom and prudence require that we have in our hands adequate means of defense. To that end, in the face of common danger, our nations are already working together, in accordance with their firmly established practice of free consultation among equals and of voluntary co-operation with regard to problems which are of common concern to all of us. It is to examine such of these problems as are immediately pressing and to seek for them most effective solutions that the representatives of the twenty-one American republics have come together at this time.
. . .

I

The war in Europe has seriously interfered with the free movement of goods in international trade. Foreign trade is much less than normal. Let us, therefore, trade with one another as much as possible and thereby, to some extent, make up for losses resulting from the falling off in European trade.

In the meantime the American nations must and should do everything in their power to strengthen their own economic position, to improve further the trade and other economic relations between and among themselves, and to devise and apply appropriate means of effective action to cope with the difficulties, disadvantages, and dangers of the present disturbed and dislocated world conditions. To accomplish these purposes the nations of the Western Hemisphere should undertake the fullest measure of economic co-operation, so designed and so conducted as to serve the best interests of each nation and to bring injury to none. . . .

II

There are those among us today who, protected by the right of freedom of speech and the right to assemble, are attempting to undermine the faith of our people in democracy, and thus to destroy it. Let us be on our guard against the "fifth column."

The solution of our economic problems alone is not

enough to preserve the peace and security of this hemisphere. There exist also other problems, which are of an altogether different character, but the solution of which is of no less importance to our freedom and independence.

I refer to the threat to our security arising from activities directed from without the hemisphere but which operate within our respective borders. A new and evil technique has been invented which seeks by devious methods to corrupt the body politic in order to subject it to alien purposes. With cynical effrontery, sanctuary within the generous citadels of free speech and freedom of assembly is demanded by agents whose masters would obliterate those institutions and foment instead dissension, prejudice, fear, and hatred.

Make no mistake concerning the purposes of this sinister campaign. It is an attempt to acquire domination of the American republics by foreign governments in their own interests.

III

What of the European possessions in the Western Hemisphere? Let us work together as guardians of those territories, keeping in mind, however, that by so doing our own interests and security must be safeguarded.

Specifically there is before us the problem of the status of the European possessions in this hemisphere.

. . . Any effort, therefore, to modify the existing status of these areas—whether by cession, by transfer, or by any impairment whatsoever in the control theretofore exercised—would be of profound and immediate concern to all the American republics.

It is accordingly essential that we consider a joint approach to this common problem. We must be in a position to move rapidly and without hesitation.

It has been suggested that our action take the form of the establishment of a collective trusteeship, to be exercised in the name of all the American republics. The Government of the United States endorses this suggestion and is prepared to co-operate, should occasion arise, in its execution. . . .

The purpose of a collective trusteeship must be to further the interests and security of all the American nations, as well as the interest of the region in question.

IV

We are facing a situation today in the causes of which we had no part. We desire to remain at peace. But let us profit by the experience of others and take all possible measures for defense.

We have met to consult together regarding our own pressing problems. We covet nothing anywhere in the world. We are free from the spirit of enmity toward any nation. But we cannot fail to be acutely conscious of the dangers which confront us as a result of present world conditions and against which we are taking and intend to take fully adequate measures of defense. . . .

Let no man say in the world of today that any nation not willing to defend itself is safe. The fortitude and resolution of our forefathers won for us our free institutions. We proudly have inherited them and proudly are prepared to defend them. . . .

Mankind can advance only when human freedom is secure; when the right of self-government is safeguarded; when all nations recognize each other's right to conduct its internal affairs free from outside interference; when there exist among nations respect for the pledged word, determination to abstain from the use of armed force in pursuit of policy, and willingness to settle controversies by none but peaceful means; when international economic relations are based upon mutual benefit, equality of treatment, and fair dealing.

In 1937, in an attempt to prevent the impending catastrophe of a new war, the Government of the United States addressed a communication to all nations, reciting these basic principles of orderly international relations under the rule of law as the foundation of its foreign policy and inviting comment thereon. More than fifty nations expressed on that occasion their belief in the validity of these principles. At Montevideo, at Buenos Aires, at Lima, at Panama, the twenty-one American republics proclaimed their acceptance.

I am confident that, sooner or later, the entire world must return to a system of international relations based on those principles. They are the only possible foundation stones of an organized society assured of enduring peace and sustained prosperity. The price of their abandonment is the chaos of international anarchy and the inexorable impoverishment of nations and individuals such as we witness today in Europe and Asia.

In a system of co-operative peace such as we envisage there is no exclusion. Its underlying principles are universal in their applicability. They can be accepted by all nations to the benefit of each and all. They must be accepted by all if the light of modern civilization is not to be extinguished. Any nation which in good faith accepts and practices them automatically shares in the vast benefits they confer.

At this time, when these principles and these ideals are being widely challenged, when institutions based on them are being crushed by force over large areas of the world, it is doubly essential that our nations keep them alive and rededicate themselves to the cause of their preservation.

It is in this spirit, and in this spirit alone, that the government which I have the honor to represent approaches the tasks that are before our present meeting—in complete confidence that in this vital respect all of the American nations stand today as united as ever.

FRANKLIN DELANO ROOSEVELT

To President Franklin D. Roosevelt fell the responsibility of piloting our country during the years of the second World War. His "Good Neighbor" policy has helped to unite the American republics against the "new order" of the dictators.

PRESIDENT ROOSEVELT'S DEFIANCE OF THE DICTATORS

Franklin D. Roosevelt became President of the United States in 1933—the same year in which Adolf Hitler seized the government of Germany, the twelfth year of Benito Mussolini's power in Italy. Roosevelt was re-elected in 1936 at a time when foreign affairs were becoming increasingly troublesome.

President Roosevelt's second term of office saw the destruction of democratic government in many European countries as the armies of the dictators overran the continent. In our own country public opinion strongly condemned the dictators and sympathized with the nations which had dared to resist.

On December 29, 1940, President Roosevelt delivered a radio talk to the nation. This speech gave fully the reasons why our government was willing to do everything in its power, short of actual war, to help the democracies which were fighting for their lives.

FROM PRESIDENT ROOSEVELT'S SPEECH OF DECEMBER 29, 1940

MY FRIENDS:

This is not a fireside chat on war. It is a talk on national security; because the nub of the whole purpose of your President is to keep you now, and your children later, and your grandchildren much later, out of a last-ditch war for the preservation of American independence and all of the things that American independence means to you and to me and to ours.

. . .

Never before since Jamestown and Plymouth Rock has our American civilization been in such danger as now.

For on September 27, 1940—this year—by an agreement signed in Berlin, three powerful nations, two in Europe and one in Asia, joined themselves together in the threat that if the United States of America interfered with or blocked the expansion program of these three nations—a program aimed at world control—they would unite in ultimate action against the United States.

The Nazi masters of Germany have made it clear that they intend not only to dominate all life and thought in their own country, but also to enslave the whole of Europe, and then to use the resources of Europe to dominate the rest of the world.

It was only three weeks ago that their leader stated this: "There are two worlds that stand opposed to each other."   And then in defiant reply to his opponents he said this: "Others are correct when they say: 'With this world we cannot ever reconcile ourselves.'   I can beat any other power in the world." So said the leader of the Nazis.

In other words, the Axis not merely admits, but the Axis proclaims, that there can be no ultimate peace between their philosophy—their philosophy of government—and our philosophy of government.

In view of the nature of this undeniable threat, it can be asserted, properly and categorically, that the United States has no right or reason to encourage talk of peace until the day shall come when there is a clear intention on the part of the aggressor nations to abandon all thought of dominating or conquering the world.

At this moment the forces of the States that are leagued against all peoples who live in freedom are being held away from our shores. The Germans and the Italians are being blocked on the other side of the Atlantic by the British and by the Greeks, and by thousands of soldiers and sailors who were able to escape from subjugated countries. In Asia the Japanese are being engaged by the Chinese nation in another great defense.

In the Pacific Ocean is our fleet.

Some of our people like to believe that wars in Europe and in Asia are of no concern to us. But it is a matter of most vital concern to us that European and Asiatic war-makers should not gain control of the oceans which lead to this hemisphere.

One hundred and seventeen years ago the Monroe Doctrine was conceived by our government as a measure of defense in the face of a threat against this hemisphere by an alliance in Continental Europe. Thereafter, we stood guard in the Atlantic with the British as neighbors. There was no treaty. There was no "unwritten agreement."

And yet there was the feeling, proven correct by

history, that we as neighbors could settle any disputes in peaceful fashion. And the fact is that during the whole of this time the Western Hemisphere has remained free from aggression from Europe or from Asia.

Does anyone seriously believe that we need to fear attack anywhere in the Americas while a free Britain remains our most powerful naval neighbor in the Atlantic? And does anyone seriously believe, on the other hand, that we could rest easy if the Axis powers were our neighbors there?

If Great Britain goes down, the Axis powers will control the continents of Europe, Asia, Africa, Australasia, and the high seas—and they will be in a position to bring enormous military and naval resources against this hemisphere. It is no exaggeration to say that all of us in all the Americas would be living at the point of a gun—a gun loaded with explosive bullets, economic as well as military.

We should enter upon a new and terrible era in which the whole world, our hemisphere included, would be run by threats of brute force. And to survive in such a world, we would have to convert ourselves permanently into a militaristic power on the basis of war economy.

Some of us like to believe that even if Britain falls we are still safe, because of the broad expanse of the Atlantic and of the Pacific.

But the width of those oceans is not what it was in the days of the clipper ships. . . . Why, even today we have planes that could fly from the British Isles to New England and back again without refueling.   And remember that the range of the modern bomber is ever being increased. . . .

Frankly and definitely, there is danger ahead—danger against which we must prepare.   But we well know that we cannot escape danger, or the fear of danger, by crawling into bed and pulling the covers over our heads.

Some nations of Europe were bound by solemn non-intervention pacts with Germany.   Other nations were assured by Germany that they need never fear invasion.   Non-intervention pact or not, the fact remains that they were attacked, overrun, thrown into modern slavery at an hour's notice, or even without any notice at all. . . .

The Nazis have justified such actions by various pious frauds.   One of these frauds is the claim that they are occupying the nation for the purpose of "restoring order."   Another is that they are occupying or controlling a nation on the excuse that they are "protecting it" against the aggression of somebody else.

For example, Germany has said that she was occupying Belgium to save the Belgians from the British.   Would she then hesitate to say to any South American country: "We are occupying you to protect you from aggression by the United States"?

Belgium today is being used as an invasion base against Britain, now fighting for its life.   And any

South American country, in Nazi hands, would always constitute a jumping-off place for German attack on any one of the other republics of this hemisphere. . . .

There are those who say that the Axis powers would never have any desire to attack the Western Hemisphere. That is the same dangerous form of wishful thinking which has destroyed the powers of resistance of so many conquered peoples. The plain facts are that the Nazis have proclaimed, time and again, that all other races are their inferiors and therefore subject to their orders. And most important of all, the vast resources and wealth of this American hemisphere constitute the most tempting loot in all of the round world. . . .

The experience of the past two years has proven beyond doubt that no nation can appease the Nazis. No man can tame a tiger into a kitten by stroking it. There can be no appeasement with ruthlessness. There can be no reasoning with an incendiary bomb. We know now that a nation can have peace with the Nazis only at the price of total surrender. . . .

The American appeasers ignore the warning to be found in the fate of Austria, Czechoslovakia, Poland, Norway, Belgium, the Netherlands, Denmark, and France. They tell you that the Axis powers are going to win anyway; that all of this bloodshed in the world could be saved; that the United States might just as well throw its influence into the scale of a dictated peace and get the best out of it that we can.

They call it a "negotiated peace." Nonsense! Is it a negotiated peace if a gang of outlaws surrounds your community and on threat of extermination makes you pay tribute to save your own skins?

Such a dictated peace would be no peace at all. It would be only another armistice, leading to the most gigantic armament race and the most devastating trade wars in all history. And in these contests the Americas would offer the only real resistance to the Axis powers. With all their vaunted efficiency, with all their parade of pious purpose in this war, there are still in their background the concentration camp and the servants of God in chains.

The history of recent years proves that the shootings and the chains and the concentration camps are not simply the transient tools but the very altars of modern dictatorships. They may talk of a "new order" in the world, but what they have in mind is only a revival of the oldest and worst tyranny. In that there is no liberty, no religion, no hope.

The proposed "new order" is the very opposite of a United States of Europe or a United States of Asia. It is not a government based upon the consent of the governed. It is not a union of ordinary, self-respecting men and women to protect themselves and their freedom and their dignity from oppression. It is an unholy alliance of power and pelf to dominate and to enslave the human race.

The British people and their allies today are conducting an active war against this unholy alliance.

Our own future security is greatly dependent on the outcome of that fight. Our ability to "keep out of war" is going to be affected by that outcome.

Thinking in terms of today and tomorrow, I make the direct statement to the American people that there is far less chance of the United States getting into war if we do all we can now to support the nations defending themselves against attack by the Axis than if we acquiesce in their defeat, submit tamely to an Axis victory, and wait our turn to be the object of attack in another war later on.

If we are to be completely honest with ourselves, we must admit that there is risk in any course we may take. But I deeply believe that the great majority of our people agree that the course that I advocate involves the least risk now and the greatest hope for world peace in the future.

The people of Europe who are defending themselves do not ask us to do their fighting. They ask us for the implements of war, the planes, the tanks, the guns, the freighters which will enable them to fight for their liberty and for our security. Emphatically, we must get these weapons to them, get them to them in sufficient volume and quickly enough so that we and our children will be saved the agony and suffering of war which others have had to endure.

Let not the defeatists tell us that it is too late. It will never be earlier. Tomorrow will be later than today.

Certain facts are self-evident.

In a military sense Great Britain and the British Empire are today the spearhead of resistance to world conquest. And they are putting up a fight which will live forever in the story of human gallantry.

There is no demand for sending an American expeditionary force outside our own borders. There is no intention by any member of your government to send such a force. You can, therefore, nail, nail any talk about sending armies to Europe as deliberate untruth.

Our national policy is not directed toward war. Its sole purpose is to keep war away from our country and away from our people.

Democracy's fight against world conquest is being greatly aided, and must be more greatly aided, by the rearmament of the United States and by sending every ounce and every ton of munitions and supplies that we can possibly spare to help the defenders who are in the front lines. And it is no more unneutral for us to do that than it is for Sweden, Russia, and other nations near Germany to send steel and ore and oil and other war materials into Germany every day in the week.

We are planning our own defense with the utmost urgency, and in its vast scale we must integrate the war needs of Britain and the other free nations which are resisting aggression.

This is not a matter of sentiment or of controversial personal opinion. It is a matter of realistic, practical military policy, based on the advice of our military experts who are in close touch with existing warfare. These military and naval experts and the members of the Congress and the Administration have a single-minded purpose—the defense of the United States.

This nation is making a great effort to produce everything that is necessary in this emergency—and with all possible speed. And this great effort requires great sacrifice. . . .

We must be the great arsenal of Democracy. For us this is an emergency as serious as war itself. We must apply ourselves to our task with the same resolution, the same sense of urgency, the same spirit of patriotism and sacrifice as we would show were we at war.

We have furnished the British great material support and we will furnish far more in the future.

There will be no "bottlenecks" in our determination to aid Great Britain. No dictator, no combination of dictators, will weaken that determination by threats of how they will construe that determination.

The British have received invaluable military support from the heroic Greek army and from the forces of all the governments in exile. Their strength is growing. It is the strength of men and women who value their freedom more highly than they value their lives.

I believe that the Axis powers are not going to win this war. I base that belief on the latest and best of information.

We have no excuse for defeatism. We have every good reason for hope—hope for peace, yes, and hope for the defense of our civilization and for the building of a better civilization in the future.

I have the profound conviction that the American people are now determined to put forth a mightier effort than they have ever yet made to increase our production of all the implements of defense, to meet the threat to our democratic faith.

As President of the United States, I call for that national effort. I call for it in the name of this nation which we love and honor and which we are privileged and proud to serve. I call upon our people with absolute confidence that our common cause will greatly succeed.

THE UNITED STATES ENTERS THE SECOND WORLD WAR

On Sunday, December 7, 1941, Japanese planes suddenly swooped down over the American territory of Hawaii and dropped bombs on the city of Honolulu and the American warships in Pearl Harbor. Our country was not at war with Japan, and the attack was totally unexpected.

All America was stunned. True, relations between Japan and the United States had been strained for some time. Our country had protested against Japan's invasion of China in 1937 because we felt that the war endangered American lives and property there. Then, in 1940, Japan joined the Axis powers and took her stand as a foe to democracy. Through the fall of France in that same year, Japan secured permission to station troops in French Indo-China. When, in 1941, she sent additional troops into French Indo-China, the United States, Great Britain, and the Netherlands stopped credit to Japan and halted exports to that nation.

Japan protested violently. She asserted that these moves were designed to ruin her. However, she sent a special emissary to Washington to discuss a peaceful settlement with our country.

Washington received the Japanese representative in good faith, and a conference including this emissary, the Japanese ambassador, and United States officials was being carried on at the very time Hawaii was attacked.

Following her treacherous attack, Japan declared war against both Great Britain and the United States.

There could be only one answer to such dishonorable tactics. On December 8, President Roosevelt asked Congress to declare that war existed between our country and Japan. The reply was swift and decisive. In little more than one hour, the Congress of the United States declared war against Japan.

PRESIDENT ROOSEVELT'S WAR MESSAGE

December 8, 1941

MR. VICE-PRESIDENT, MR. SPEAKER, MEMBERS OF THE SENATE AND OF THE HOUSE OF REPRESENTATIVES:

Yesterday, December 7, 1941—a date which will live in infamy—the United States of America was suddenly and deliberately attacked by naval and air forces of the Empire of Japan.

The United States was at peace with that nation and, at the solicitation of Japan, was still in conversation with its government and its Emperor looking toward the maintenance of peace in the Pacific.

Indeed, one hour after Japanese air squadrons had commenced bombing in the American island of Oahu, the Japanese Ambassador to the United States and his colleague delivered to our Secretary of State a formal reply to a recent American message. While this reply stated that it seemed useless to continue the existing diplomatic negotiations, it contained no threat or hint of war or armed attack.

It will be recorded that the distance of Hawaii from Japan makes it obvious that the attack was deliberately planned many days or even weeks ago. During the intervening time the Japanese government has deliberately sought to deceive the United States by false statements and expressions of hope for continued peace.

The attack yesterday on the Hawaiian Islands has caused severe damage to American naval and military forces. I regret to tell you that many American lives have been lost. In addition, American ships have been reported torpedoed on the high seas between San Francisco and Honolulu.

Yesterday the Japanese government also launched an attack against Malaya.

Last night Japanese forces attacked Hong Kong.

Last night Japanese forces attacked Guam.

Last night Japanese forces attacked the Philippine Islands.

Last night the Japanese attacked Wake Island.

And this morning the Japanese attacked Midway Island.

Japan has, therefore, undertaken a surprise offensive extending throughout the Pacific area. The facts of yesterday and today speak for themselves. The people of the United States have already formed their opinions and well understand the implications to the very life and safety of our nation.

As Commander in Chief of the Army and Navy, I have directed that all measures be taken for our defense.

Always will our whole nation remember the character of the onslaught against us.

No matter how long it may take us to overcome this premeditated invasion, the American people in their righteous might will win through to absolute victory.

I believe I interpret the will of the Congress and of the people when I assert that we will not only defend ourselves to the uttermost but will make it very certain that this form of treachery shall never again endanger us.

Hostilities exist.   There is no blinking at the fact that our people, our territory, and our interests are in grave danger.

With confidence in our armed forces—with the unbounded determination of our people—we will gain the inevitable triumph—so help us God.

I ask that the Congress declare that since the unprovoked and dastardly attack by Japan on Sunday, December 7, 1941, a state of war has existed between the United States and the Japanese Empire.

PRESIDENT ROOSEVELT'S SPEECH
TO THE NATION, DECEMBER 9, 1941

MY FELLOW-AMERICANS:

The sudden criminal attacks perpetrated by the Japanese in the Pacific provide the climax of a decade of international immorality.

Powerful and resourceful gangsters have banded together to make war upon the whole human race. Their challenge has now been flung at the United States of America. The Japanese have treacherously violated the long-standing peace between us. Many American soldiers and sailors have been killed by enemy action. American ships have been sunk; American airplanes have been destroyed.

The Congress and the people of the United States have accepted that challenge.

Together with other free peoples, we are now fighting to maintain our right to live among our world neighbors in freedom and in common decency, without fear of assault.

I have prepared the full record of our past relations with Japan, and it will be submitted to the Congress. It begins with the visit of Commodore Perry to Japan eighty-eight years ago. It ends with the visit of two Japanese emissaries to the Secretary of State last Sunday, an hour after Japanese forces had loosed their bombs and machine guns against our flag, our forces, and our citizens.

I can say with utmost confidence that no Americans today or a thousand years hence, need feel anything but pride in our patience and our efforts through all the years toward achieving a peace in the Pacific which would be fair and honorable to every nation, large or small. And no honest person, today or a thousand years hence, will be able to suppress a sense of indignation and horror at the treachery committed by the military dictators of Japan, under the very shadow of the flag of peace borne by their special envoys in our midst.

The course that Japan has followed for the past ten years in Asia has paralleled the course of Hitler and Mussolini in Europe and Africa. Today, it has become far more than a parallel. It is collaboration so well calculated that all the continents of the world, and all the oceans, are now considered by the Axis strategists as one gigantic battlefield.

In 1931, Japan invaded Manchukuo—without warning.

In 1935, Italy invaded Ethiopia—without warning.

In 1938, Hitler occupied Austria—without warning.

In 1939, Hitler invaded Czechoslovakia—without warning.

Later in 1939, Hitler invaded Poland—without warning.

In 1940, Hitler invaded Norway, Denmark, Holland, Belgium, and Luxembourg—without warning.

In 1940, Italy attacked France and later Greece—without warning.

In 1941, the Axis powers attacked Yugoslavia and Greece and they dominated the Balkans—without warning.

In 1941, Hitler invaded Russia—without warning.

And now Japan has attacked Malaya and Thailand —and the United States—without warning.

It is all of one pattern.

We are now in this war. We are in it—all the way. Every single man, woman, and child is a partner in the most tremendous undertaking of our American history. We must share together the bad news and the good news, the defeats and the victories—the changing fortunes of war.

So far, the news has all been bad. We have suffered a serious set-back in Hawaii. Our forces in the Philippines, which include the brave people of that commonwealth, are taking punishment, but are defending themselves vigorously. The reports from Guam and Wake and Midway Islands are still confused, but we must be prepared for the announcement that all these three outposts have been seized.

The casualty lists of these first few days will undoubtedly be large. I deeply feel the anxiety of all families of the men in our armed forces and the relatives of people in cities which have been bombed. I can only give them my solemn promise that they will get news just as quickly as possible.

This Government will put its trust in the stamina of the American people and will give the facts to the public as soon as two conditions have been fulfilled:

first, that the information has been definitely and officially confirmed; and, second, that the release of the information at the time it is received will not prove valuable to the enemy directly or indirectly.

Most earnestly I urge my countrymen to reject all rumors. These ugly little hints of complete disaster fly thick and fast in wartime. They have to be examined and appraised.

As an example, I can tell you frankly that until further surveys are made, I have not sufficient information to state the exact damage which has been done to our naval vessels at Pearl Harbor. Admittedly the damage is serious. But no one can say how serious until we know how much of this damage can be repaired and how quickly the necessary repairs can be made.

I cite as another example a statement made on Sunday night that a Japanese carrier had been located and sunk off the Canal Zone. And when you hear statements that are attributed to what they call "an authoritative source," you can be reasonably sure that under these war circumstances the "authoritative source" was not any person in authority.

Many rumors and reports which we now hear originate with enemy sources. For instance, today the Japanese are claiming that as a result of their one action against Hawaii they have gained naval supremacy in the Pacific. This is an old trick of propaganda which has been used innumerable times by the Nazis. The purposes of such fantastic claims are, of course, to spread fear and confusion among us, and to goad us into revealing military information which our enemies are desperately anxious to obtain.

Our government will not be caught in this obvious trap—and neither will our people.

It must be remembered by each and every one of us that our free and rapid communication must be greatly restricted in wartime. It is not possible to receive full, speedy, accurate reports from distant areas of combat. This is particularly true where naval operations are concerned. For in these days of the marvels of radio it is often impossible for the commanders of various units to report their activities by radio, for the very simple reason that this information would become available to the enemy, and would disclose their position and their plan of defense or attack.

Of necessity there will be delays in officially confirming or denying reports of operations, but we will not hide facts from the country if we know the facts and if the enemy will not be aided by their disclosure.

To all newspapers and radio stations—all those who reach the eyes and ears of the American people—I say this: You have a most grave responsibility to the nation now and for the duration of this war.

If you feel that your government is not disclosing enough of the truth, you have every right to say so. But—in the absence of all the facts, as revealed by official sources—you have no right to deal out unconfirmed reports in such a way as to make people believe they are Gospel truth.

Every citizen, in every walk of life, shares this same responsibility. The lives of our soldiers and sailors— the whole future of this nation—depend upon the manner in which each and every one of us fulfills his obligation to our country.

Now a word about the recent past—and the future. A year and a half has elapsed since the fall of France, when the whole world first realized the mechanized might which the Axis nations had been building for so many years. America has used that year and a half to great advantage. Knowing that the attack might reach us in all too short a time, we immediately began greatly to increase our industrial strength and our capacity to meet the demands of modern warfare.

Precious months were gained by sending vast quantities of our war material to the nations of the world still able to resist Axis aggression. Our policy rested on the fundamental truth that the defense of any country resisting Hitler or Japan was in the long run the defense of our own country. That policy has been justified. It has given us time, invaluable time, to build our American assembly lines of production.

Assembly lines are now in operation. Others are being rushed to completion. A steady stream of tanks and planes, of guns and ships, of shells and equipment—that is what these eighteen months have given us.

But it is all only a beginning of what has to be done.

We must be set to face a long war against crafty and powerful bandits. The attack at Pearl Harbor can be repeated at any one of many points in both oceans and along both our coast lines and against all the rest of the hemisphere.

It will not only be a long war, it will be a hard war. That is the basis on which we now lay all our plans. That is the yardstick by which we measure what we shall need and demand: money, materials, doubled and quadrupled production—ever increasing. The production must be not only for our own Army and Navy and air forces. It must reinforce the other armies and navies and air forces fighting the Nazis and the war lords of Japan throughout the Americas and the world.

I have been working today on the subject of production. Your government has decided on two broad policies.

The first is to speed up all existing production by working on a seven-day-week basis in every war industry, including the production of essential raw materials.

The second policy, now being put into form, is to rush additions to the capacity of production by building more new plants, by adding to old plants, and by using the many smaller plants for war needs.

Over the hard road of the past months we have at times met obstacles and difficulties, divisions and disputes, indifference and callousness. That is now all past—and, I am sure, forgotten.

The fact is that the country now has an organization in Washington built around men and women who are recognized experts in their own fields. I think the country knows that the people who are actually responsible in each and every one of these many fields are pulling together with a teamwork that has never before been excelled.

On the road ahead there lies hard work—gruelling work—day and night, every hour and every minute.

I was about to add that ahead there lies sacrifice for all of us.

But it is not correct to use that word. The United States does not consider it a sacrifice to do all one can, to give one's best to our nation, when the nation is fighting for its existence and its future life.

It is not a sacrifice for any man, old or young, to be in the Army or the Navy of the United States. Rather is it a privilege.

It is not a sacrifice for the industrialist or the wage-earner, the farmer or the shopkeeper, the trainman or the doctor, to pay more taxes, to buy more bonds, to forego extra profits, to work longer or harder at the task for which he is best fitted. Rather is it a privilege.

It is not a sacrifice to do without many things to which we are accustomed if the national defense calls for doing without.

A review this morning leads me to the conclusion that at present we shall not have to curtail the normal articles of food. There is enough food for all of us and enough left over to send to those who are fighting on the same side with us.

There will be a clear and definite shortage of metals of many kinds for civilian use, for the very good reason that in our increased program we shall need for war purposes more than half of that portion of the principal metals which during the past year have gone into articles for civilian use. We shall have to give up many things entirely.

I am sure that the people in every part of the nation are prepared in their individual living to win this war. I am sure they will cheerfully help to pay a large part of its financial cost while it goes on. I am sure they will cheerfully give up those material things they are asked to give up.

I am sure that they will retain all those great spiritual things without which we cannot win through.

I repeat that the United States can accept no result save victory, final and complete. Not only must the shame of Japanese treachery be wiped out, but the sources of international brutality, wherever they exist, must be absolutely and finally broken.

In my message to the Congress yesterday I said that we "will make very certain that this form of treachery shall never endanger us again." In order to achieve that certainty, we must begin the great task that is before us by abandoning once and for all the illusion that we can ever again isolate ourselves from the rest of humanity.

In these past few years—and, most violently, in

the past few days—we have learned a terrible lesson. It is our obligation to our dead—it is our sacred obligation to their children and our children—that we must never forget what we have learned.

And what we all have learned is this:

There is no such thing as security for any nation— or any individual—in a world ruled by the principles of gangsterism.

There is no such thing as impregnable defense against powerful aggressors who sneak up in the dark and strike without warning.

We have learned that our ocean-girt hemisphere is not immune from severe attack—that we cannot measure our safety in terms of miles on any map.

We may acknowledge that our enemies have performed a brilliant feat of deception, perfectly timed and executed with great skill. It was a thoroughly dishonorable deed, but we must face the fact that modern warfare as conducted in the Nazi manner is a dirty business. We don't like it—we didn't want to get in it—but we are in it and we're going to fight it with everything we've got.

I do not think any American has any doubt of our ability to administer proper punishment to the perpetrators of these crimes.

Your Government knows that for weeks Germany has been telling Japan that if Japan did not attack the United States, Japan would not share in dividing the spoils with Germany when peace came. She was promised by Germany that if she came in she would receive the complete and perpetual control of the whole of the Pacific area—and that means not only the Far East, not only all of the islands in the Pacific, but also a stranglehold on the west coast of North, Central, and South America.

We also know that Germany and Japan are conducting their military and naval operations in accordance with a joint plan. That plan considers all peoples and nations which are not helping the Axis powers as common enemies of each and every one of the Axis powers.

That is their simple and obvious grand strategy. That is why the American people must realize that it can be matched only with similar grand strategy.

We must realize, for example, that Japanese successes against the United States in the Pacific are helpful to German operations in Libya; that any German success against the Caucasus is inevitably an assistance to Japan in her operations against the Dutch East Indies; that a German attack against Algiers or Morocco opens the way to a German attack against South America.

On the other side of the picture, we must learn to know that guerilla warfare against the Germans in Serbia helps us; that a successful Russian offensive against the Germans helps us; and that British successes on land or sea in any part of the world strengthen our hands.

Remember always that Germany and Italy, regardless of any formal declaration of war, consider themselves at war with the United States at this moment just as much as they consider themselves at war with Britain and Russia. And Germany puts all the other republics of the Americas into the category of enemies. The people of the hemisphere can be honored by that.

The true goal we seek is far above and beyond the ugly field of battle. When we resort to force, as now we must, we are determined that this force shall be directed toward ultimate good as well as against immediate evil. We Americans are not destroyers—we are builders.

We are now in the midst of a war, not for conquest, not for vengeance, but for a world in which this nation, and all that this nation represents, will be safe for our children. We expect to eliminate the danger from Japan, but it would serve us ill if we accomplished that and found that the rest of the world was dominated by Hitler and Mussolini.

We are going to win the war and we are going to win the peace that follows.

And in the dark hours of this day—and through dark days that may be yet to come—we will know that the vast majority of the members of the human race are on our side. Many of them are fighting with us. All of them are praying for us. For, in representing our cause, we represent theirs as well—our hope and their hope for liberty under God.

AT WAR WITH GERMANY AND ITALY

Claiming their action was in fulfillment of their alliance with Japan, Germany and Italy declared war against the United States on December 11, 1941.

Within a very few hours Congress, at the suggestion of the President, had replied in kind, and the President signed the war declarations. The two were the same except that one named Germany and the other named Italy.

OUR DECLARATION OF WAR

Whereas the government of Germany has formally declared war against the Government and the people of the United States of America:

Therefore, be it

Resolved by the Senate and House of Representatives of the United States of America in Congress assembled, that the state of war between the United States and the government of Germany which has thus been thrust upon the United States is hereby formally declared; and the President is hereby authorized and directed to employ the entire naval and military forces of the United States and the resources of the Government to carry on war against the government of Germany; and, to bring the conflict to a successful termination, all of the resources of the country are hereby pledged by the Congress of the United States.

IS DEMOCRACY WORTH FIGHTING FOR?

What are the blessings of Democracy that make it more desirable than other forms of government? Let us see what our American Democracy offers to the people who live under its rule.

1. Equal opportunity and equal rights, regardless of race, creed, position, or wealth.
2. The right of self government through the election of our own representatives to make and enforce our laws.
3. Freedom of speech, freedom of the press, freedom of assembly, freedom of religion, and freedom to live our lives in our own way subject to our own restrictions according to our own laws.
4. Protection from aggression.
5. Free education.
6. High standards of living.
7. Trial by jury.
8. Economic security for the needy and unemployed.
9. Freedom from persecution and from seizure of private property.
10. The right to work changes in conditions which do not seem to benefit a portion of the people.

We who are citizens of the United States or who live under its protection owe absolute loyalty to its government. What are some of our obligations to it?

1. Obedience to its laws.

2. Payment of our proportionate share of the cost of government and general welfare.
3. Willingness to sacrifice our personal feelings or prejudices for the good of the majority.
4. Observance of our duties as citizens, in upholding the laws and working for the common good.
5. The responsibility of becoming educated and well-informed so that we may vote wisely in the election of our representatives and the passing of our laws.
6. Loyal service in times of need.
7. Wise use of the liberties which are granted us.
8. Respect for the democratic form of government and defense of it when it is the subject of attack.

Can you imagine what it would be like to live in a dictator-ruled country; to be afraid to criticize the acts of its ruler for fear of your very life; to know that everything you work for and possess may be taken from you; to have no part in your own government; to be unable to worship or live as you please? As American citizens we should strive to see that *government of the people, by the people, for the people, shall not perish from the earth,* for without it we should return to the dark days when men were slaves of their masters and freedom for the individual was unknown.

LOYALTY TO FLAG AND COUNTRY

The sight of the American flag and the thought of what it stands for are enough to thrill the heart of every true American. The Pledge of Allegiance to the flag has a deep significance, especially at a time when Liberty is endangered throughout the world.

THE PLEDGE OF ALLEGIANCE

I pledge allegiance to the Flag of the United States of America and to the Republic for which it stands, one Nation, indivisible, with Liberty and Justice for all.

In 1917, William Tyler Page, Clerk of the House of Representatives, wrote The American's Creed, which was accepted by the House the following year in behalf of the American people.

THE AMERICAN'S CREED

WILLIAM TYLER PAGE

I believe in the United States of America as a Government of the people, by the people, for the people, whose just powers are derived from the consent of the governed; a democracy in a republic; a sovereign Nation of many sovereign States; a perfect Union, one and inseparable; established upon those principles of freedom, equality, justice, and humanity for which American patriots sacrificed their lives and fortunes.

I therefore believe it is my duty to my country to love it; to support its Constitution; to obey its laws; to respect its flag; and to defend it against all enemies.

TRUE PATRIOTISM

Sir Walter Scott

Breathes there the man with soul so dead,
Who never to himself hath said,
　"This is my own, my native land!"
Whose heart hath ne'er within him burned,
As home his footsteps he hath turned
　From wandering on a foreign strand?
If such there breathes, go, mark him well;
For him no minstrel raptures swell.
High though his titles, proud his name,
Boundless his wealth as wish can claim,
Despite those titles, power and pelf,
The wretch, concentered all in self,
Living, shall forfeit fair renown,
And, doubly dying, shall go down
To the vile dust from which he sprung,
Unwept, unhonored, and unsung.

GOD BLESS AMERICA

A Patriotic Song by Irving Berlin

God bless America,
　Land that I love,
Stand beside her
　And guide her
Through the night
　By the light from above;
From the mountains,
　And the prairies,
To the ocean white with foam,
　God bless America,
　　Our home sweet home.
　God bless America,
　　Our home sweet home.

THE OLD FLAG FOREVER

Frank L. Stanton

She's up there—Old Glory—where lightnings are
　sped;
She dazzles the nations with ripples of red;
And she'll wave for us living, or droop o'er us dead—
　The flag of our country forever!

She's up there—Old Glory—how bright the stars
    stream!
And the stripes like red signals of liberty gleam!
And we dare for her, living, or dream the last dream
    'Neath the flag of our country forever!

She's up there—Old Glory—no tyrant-dealt scars
Nor blur on her brightness, no stain on her stars!
The brave blood of heroes hath crimsoned her bars.
    She's the flag of our country forever!

APPENDIX

THE CONSTITUTION OF THE UNITED STATES

Which went into effect March 4, 1789

We, the People of the United States, in order to form a more perfect union, establish justice, insure domestic tranquillity, provide for the common defence, promote the general welfare, and secure the blessings of liberty to ourselves and our posterity, do ordain and establish this CONSTITUTION for the United States of America.

ARTICLE I

SECTION 1. All legislative powers herein granted shall be vested in a Congress of the United States, which shall consist of a Senate and House of Representatives.

SECTION 2. The House of Representatives shall be composed of members chosen every second year by the people of the several States, and the electors in each State shall have the qualifications requisite for electors of the most numerous branch of the State Legislature.

No person shall be a representative who shall not have attained to the age of twenty-five years, and been seven years a citizen of the United States, and who shall not, when elected, be an inhabitant of that State in which he shall be chosen.

Representatives and direct taxes shall be apportioned among the several States which may be included within this Union, according to their respective numbers, which shall be determined by adding to the whole number of free persons, including those bound to service for a term of years, and excluding Indians not taxed, three-fifths of all other persons.

The actual enumeration shall be made within three years after the first meeting of the Congress of the United States, and within every subsequent term of ten years, in such manner as they shall by law direct. The number of representatives shall not exceed one for every thirty thousand, but each State shall have at least one representative: and until such enumeration shall be made, the State of New Hampshire shall be entitled to choose three; Massachusetts, eight; Rhode Island and Providence Plantations, one; Connecticut, five; New York, six; New Jersey, four; Pennsylvania, eight; Delaware, one; Maryland, six; Virginia, ten; North Carolina, five; South Carolina, five; and Georgia, three.

When vacancies happen in the representation from any State, the executive authority thereof shall issue writs of election to fill such vacancies.

The House of Representatives shall choose their Speaker and other officers; and shall have the sole power of impeachment.

SECTION 3. The Senate of the United States shall be composed of two senators from each State, chosen by the Legislature thereof, for six years; and each senator shall have one vote.

Immediately after they shall be assembled in consequence of the first election, they shall be divided as equally as may be into three classes. The seats of the senators of the first class shall be vacated at the expiration of the second year; of the second class, at the expiration of the fourth year; of the third class, at the expiration of the sixth year, so that one-third may be chosen every second year; and if vacancies happen by resignation, or otherwise, during the recess of the Legislature of any State, the executive thereof may make temporary appointments until the next meeting of the Legislature, which shall then fill such vacancies.

No person shall be a senator who shall not have attained to the age of thirty years, and been nine years a citizen of the

United States, and who shall not, when elected, be an inhabitant of that State for which he shall be chosen.

The Vice-President of the United States shall be president of the Senate, but shall have no vote, unless they be equally divided.

The Senate shall choose their other officers, and also a president *pro tempore*, in the absence of the Vice-President, or when he shall exercise the office of President of the United States.

The Senate shall have the sole power to try all impeachments: When sitting for that purpose, they shall be on oath or affirmation. When the President of the United States is tried, the Chief-Justice shall preside; and no person shall be convicted without the concurrence of two-thirds of the members present.

Judgment in cases of impeachment shall not extend further than to removal from office, and disqualification to hold and enjoy any office of honor, trust, or profit under the United States; but the party convicted shall nevertheless be liable and subject to indictment, trial, judgment, and punishment, according to law.

SECTION 4. The times, places, and manner of holding elections for senators and representatives shall be prescribed in each State by the Legislature thereof; but the Congress may at any time, by law, make or alter such regulations, except as to the places of choosing senators.

The Congress shall assemble at least once in every year, and such meeting shall be on the first Monday in December, unless they shall by law appoint a different day.

SECTION 5. Each house shall be the judge of the elections, returns, and qualifications of its own members, and a majority of each shall constitute a quorum to do business; but a smaller number may adjourn from day to day, and may be authorized to compel the attendance of absent members, in such manner, and under such penalties, as each house may provide.

Each house may determine the rules of its proceedings,

punish its members for disorderly behavior, and, with the concurrence of two-thirds, expel a member.

Each house shall keep a journal of its proceedings, and from time to time publish the same, excepting such parts as may in their judgment require secrecy, and the yeas and nays of the members of either house on any question shall, at the desire of one-fifth of those present, be entered on the journal.

Neither house, during the session of Congress, shall, without the consent of the other, adjourn for more than three days, nor to any other place than that in which the two houses shall be sitting.

SECTION 6. The senators and representatives shall receive a compensation for their services, to be ascertained by law, and paid out of the treasury of the United States. They shall in all cases, except treason, felony, and breach of the peace, be privileged from arrest during their attendance at the session of their respective houses, and in going to and returning from the same; and for any speech or debate in either house, they shall not be questioned in any other place.

No senator or representative shall, during the time for which he was elected, be appointed to any civil office under the authority of the United States, which shall have been created, or the emoluments whereof shall have been increased, during such time; and no person holding any office under the United States shall be a member of either house during his continuance in office.

SECTION 7. All bills for raising revenue shall originate in the House of Representatives; but the Senate may propose or concur with amendments as on other bills.

Every bill which shall have passed the House of Representatives and the Senate, shall, before it become a law, be presented to the President of the United States; if he approve, he shall sign it, but if not, he shall return it, with his objections, to that house in which it shall have originated, who shall enter the objections at large on their journal, and proceed to reconsider it. If after such reconsideration, two-thirds of that house shall agree to pass the bill, it shall be sent, together with the objections, to the other house, by which it shall likewise be reconsidered, and if approved by two-thirds of that house, it shall become a law. But in all such cases the votes of both houses shall be determined by yeas and nays, and the names of the persons voting for and against the bill shall be entered on the journal of each house respectively. If any bill shall not be returned by the President within ten days (Sunday excepted) after it shall have been presented to him, the same shall be a law, in like manner as if he had signed it, unless the Congress by their adjournment prevent its return, in which case it shall not be a law.

Every order, resolution, or vote to which the concurrence of the Senate and House of Representatives may be necessary (except on a question of adjournment) shall be presented to the President of the United States; and before the same shall take effect, shall be approved by him, or being disapproved by him, shall be repassed by two-thirds of the Senate and House of Representatives, according to the rules and limitations prescribed in the case of a bill.

SECTION 8. The Congress shall have power to lay and collect taxes, duties, imposts, and excises, to pay the debts and provide for the common defence and general welfare of the United States; but all duties, imposts, and excises shall be uniform throughout the United States;

To borrow money on the credit of the United States;

To regulate commerce with foreign nations, and among the several States, and with the Indian tribes;

To establish a uniform rule of naturalization, and uniform laws on the subject of bankruptcies throughout the United States;

To coin money, regulate the value thereof, and of foreign coin, and fix the standard of weights and measures;

To provide for the punishment of counterfeiting the securities and current coin of the United States;

To establish post-offices and post-roads;

To promote the progress of science and useful arts, by securing, for limited times, to authors and inventors the exclusive right to their respective writings and discoveries;

To constitute tribunals inferior to the Supreme Court;

To define and punish piracies and felonies committed on the high seas, and offences against the law of nations;

To declare war, grant letters of marque and reprisal, and make rules concerning captures on land and water;

To raise and support armies, but no appropriation of money to that use shall be for a longer term than two years;

To provide and maintain a navy;

To make rules for the government and regulation of the land and naval forces;

To provide for calling forth the militia to execute the laws of the Union, suppress insurrections and repel invasions;

To provide for organizing, arming, and disciplining the militia, and for governing such part of them as may be employed in the service of the United States, reserving to the States respectively the appointment of the officers, and the authority of training the militia according to the discipline prescribed by Congress;

To exercise exclusive legislation in all cases whatsoever over such district (not exceeding ten miles square) as may, by cession of particular States, and the acceptance of Congress, become the seat of the government of the United States, and to exercise like authority over all places purchased by the consent of the Legislature of the State in which the same shall be, for the erection of forts, magazines, arsenals, dockyards, and other needful buildings;—And

To make all laws which shall be necessary and proper for carrying into execution the foregoing powers, and all other powers vested by this Constitution in the government of the United States, or in any department or officer thereof.

SECTION 9. The migration or importation of such persons

as any of the States now existing shall think proper to admit shall not be prohibited by the Congress prior to the year one thousand eight hundred and eight, but a tax or duty may be imposed on such importation, not exceeding ten dollars for each person.

The privilege of the writ of habeas corpus shall not be suspended, unless when in cases of rebellion or invasion the public safety may require it.

No bill of attainder or ex-post-facto law shall be passed.

No capitation or other direct tax shall be laid, unless in proportion to the census or enumeration herein before directed to be taken.

No tax or duty shall be laid on articles exported from any State.

No preference shall be given by any regulation of commerce or revenue to the ports of one State over those of another; nor shall vessels bound to, or from, one State, be obliged to enter, clear, or pay duties in another.

No money shall be drawn from the treasury but in consequence of appropriations made by law; and a regular statement and account of the receipts and expenditures of all public money shall be published from time to time.

No title of nobility shall be granted by the United States; and no person holding any office of profit or trust under them, shall, without the consent of the Congress, accept of any present, emolument, office, or title, of any kind whatever, from any king, prince, or foreign state.

SECTION 10. No State shall enter into any treaty, alliance, or confederation; grant letters of marque and reprisal; coin money; emit bills of credit; make anything but gold and silver coin a tender in payment of debts; pass any bill of attainder, ex-post-facto law, or law impairing the obligation of contracts, or grant any title of nobility.

No State shall, without the consent of the Congress, lay any impost or duties on imports or exports, except what may be absolutely necessary for executing its inspection laws; and the net produce of all duties and imposts, laid by any State on imports or exports, shall be for the use of the treasury of the United States; and all such laws shall be subject to the revision and control of the Congress.

No State shall, without the consent of Congress, lay any duty of tonnage, keep troops, or ships-of-war, in time of peace, enter into any agreement or compact with another State, or with a foreign power, or engage in war, unless actually invaded, or in such imminent danger as will not admit of delay.

ARTICLE II

SECTION 1. The executive power shall be vested in a President of the United States of America. He shall hold his office during the term of four years, and, together with the Vice-President, chosen for the same term, be elected, as follows:

Each State shall appoint, in such manner as the Legislature thereof may direct, a number of electors, equal to the whole number of senators and representatives to which the State may be entitled in the Congress; but no senator or representative, or person holding an office of trust or profit under the United States, shall be appointed an elector.

[*The electors shall meet in their respective States, and vote by ballot for two persons, of whom one at least shall not be an inhabitant of the same State with themselves. And they shall make a list of all the persons voted for, and of the number of votes for each; which list they shall sign and certify and transmit sealed to the seat of the government of the United States, directed to the president of the Senate. The president of the Senate shall, in the presence of the Senate and House of Representatives, open all the certificates, and the votes shall then be counted. The person having the greatest number of votes shall be the President, if such number be a majority of

*This paragraph has been superseded by Amendment XII.

the whole number of electors appointed; and if there be more than one who have such majority, and have an equal number of votes, then the House of Representatives shall immediately choose by ballot one of them for President; and if no person have a majority, then from the five highest on the list the said house shall, in like manner, choose the President. But in choosing the President, the votes shall be taken by States, the representation from each State having one vote; a quorum for this purpose shall consist of a member or members from two-thirds of the States, and a majority of all the States shall be necessary to a choice. In every case, after the choice of the President, the person having the greatest number of votes of the electors shall be the Vice-President. But if there should remain two or more who have equal votes, the Senate shall choose from them by ballot the Vice-President.]

The Congress may determine the time of choosing the electors, and the day on which they shall give their votes; which day shall be the same throughout the United States.

No person except a natural born citizen, or a citizen of the United States at the time of the adoption of this Constitution, shall be eligible to the office of President; neither shall any person be eligible to that office who shall not have attained to the age of thirty-five years, and been fourteen years resident within the United States.

In case of the removal of the President from office, or of his death, resignation, or inability to discharge the powers and duties of the said office, the same shall devolve on the Vice-President, and the Congress may by law provide for the case of removal, death, resignation, or inability, both of the President and Vice-President, declaring what officer shall then act as President; and such officer shall act accordingly until the disability be removed, or a President shall be elected.

The President shall, at stated times, receive for his services a compensation which shall neither be increased nor diminished during the period for which he shall have been elected, and he shall not receive within that period any other emolument from the United States, or any of them.

Before he enter on the execution of his office, he shall take the following oath or affirmation:—"I do solemnly swear (or affirm) that I will faithfully execute the office of President of the United States, and will, to the best of my ability, preserve, protect, and defend the Constitution of the United States."

SECTION 2. The President shall be commander-in-chief of the army and navy of the United States, and of the militia of the several States, when called into the actual service of the United States; he may require the opinion, in writing, of the principal officer in each of the executive departments, upon any subject relating to the duties of their respective offices; and he shall have power to grant reprieves and pardons for offences against the United States, except in cases of impeachment.

He shall have power, by and with the advice and consent of the Senate, to make treaties, provided two-thirds of the senators present concur; and he shall nominate, and by and with the advice and consent of the Senate shall appoint ambassadors, other public ministers and consuls, judges of the Supreme Court, and all other officers of the United States, whose appointments are not herein otherwise provided for, and which shall be established by law: but the Congress may by law vest the appointment of such inferior officers, as they think proper, in the President alone, in the courts of law, or in the heads of departments.

The President shall have power to fill up all vacancies that may happen during the recess of the Senate, by granting commissions which shall expire at the end of their next session.

SECTION 3. He shall from time to time give to the Congress information of the state of the Union, and recommend to their consideration such measures as he shall judge necessary and expedient; he may, on extraordinary occasions, convene both houses, or either of them, and in case of disagreement between them with respect to the time of adjournment, he may adjourn them to such time as he shall think proper; he shall receive ambassadors and other public ministers; he shall take care that the laws be faithfully executed, and shall commission all the officers of the United States.

SECTION 4. The President, Vice-President, and all civil officers of the United States, shall be removed from office on impeachment for, and conviction of, treason, bribery, or other high crimes and misdemeanors.

ARTICLE III

SECTION 1. The judicial power of the United States shall be vested in one Supreme Court, and in such inferior courts as the Congress may from time to time ordain and establish. The judges, both of the Supreme and inferior courts, shall hold their offices during good behavior, and shall, at stated times, receive for their services a compensation which shall not be diminished during their continuance in office.

SECTION 2. The judicial power shall extend to all cases, in law and equity, arising under this Constitution, the laws of the United States, and treaties made, or which shall be made, under their authority;—to all cases affecting ambassadors, other public ministers, and consuls;—to all cases of admiralty and maritime jurisdiction;—to controversies to which the United States shall be a party;—to controversies between two or more States;—between a State and citizens of another State;—between citizens of different States;—between citizens of the same State claiming lands under grants of different States; and between a State, or the citizens thereof, and foreign states, citizens, or subjects.

In all cases affecting ambassadors, other public ministers and consuls, and those in which a State shall be party, the Supreme Court shall have original jurisdiction. In all other cases before mentioned, the Supreme Court shall have appellate jurisdiction, both as to law and fact, with such exceptions and under such regulations as the Congress shall make.

The trial of all crimes, except in cases of impeachment, shall be by jury; and such trial shall be held in the State where the said crimes shall have been committed; but when not committed within any State, the trial shall be at such place or places as the Congress may by law have directed.

SECTION 3. Treason against the United States shall consist only in levying war against them, or in adhering to their enemies, giving them aid and comfort.

No person shall be convicted of treason unless on the testimony of two witnesses to the same overt act, or on confession in open court.

The Congress shall have power to declare the punishment of treason, but no attainder of treason shall work corruption of blood, or forfeiture, except during the life of the person attainted.

ARTICLE IV

SECTION 1. Full faith and credit shall be given in each State to the public acts, records, and judicial proceedings of every other State. And the Congress may, by general laws, prescribe the manner in which such acts, records, and proceedings shall be proved, and the effect thereof.

SECTION 2. The citizens of each State shall be entitled to all privileges and immunities of citizens in the several States.

A person charged in any State with treason, felony, or other crime, who shall flee from justice, and be found in another State, shall, on demand of the executive authority of the State from which he fled, be delivered up, to be removed to the State having jurisdiction of the crime.

No person held to service or labor in one State, under the laws thereof, escaping into another, shall, in consequence of any law or regulation therein, be discharged from such service or labor, but shall be delivered up on claim of the party to whom such service or labor may be due.

SECTION 3. New States may be admitted by the Congress into this Union; but no new State shall be formed or erected within the jurisdiction of any other State; nor any State be formed by the junction of two or more States, or parts of States, without the consent of the Legislatures of the States concerned as well as of the Congress.

The Congress shall have power to dispose of and make all needful rules and regulations respecting the territory or other property belonging to the United States; and nothing in this Constitution shall be so construed as to prejudice any claims of the United States, or of any particular State.

SECTION 4. The United States shall guarantee to every State in this Union a republican form of government, and shall protect each of them against invasion, and on application of the Legislature, or of the Executive (when the Legislature cannot be convened) against domestic violence.

ARTICLE V

The Congress, whenever two-thirds of both houses shall deem it necessary, shall propose amendments to this Constitution, or, on the application of the Legislatures of two-thirds of the several States, shall call a convention for proposing amendments, which, in either case, shall be valid to all intents and purposes, as part of this Constitution, when ratified by the Legislatures of three-fourths of the several States, or by conventions in three-fourths thereof, as the one or the other mode of ratification may be proposed by the Congress; provided that no amendment which may be made prior to the year one thousand eight hundred and eight shall in any manner affect the first and fourth clauses in the ninth section of the first article; and that no State, without its consent, shall be deprived of its equal suffrage in the Senate.

ARTICLE VI

All debts contracted, and engagements entered into, before the adoption of this Constitution, shall be as valid against the United States under this Constitution, as under the Confederation.

This Constitution, and the laws of the United States which shall be made in pursuance thereof; and all treaties made, or which shall be made, under the authority of the United States, shall be the supreme law of the land; and the judges in every State shall be bound thereby, anything in the Constitution or laws of any State to the contrary notwithstanding.

The senators and representatives before mentioned, and the members of the several State Legislatures, and all executive and judicial officers, both of the United States and of the several States, shall be bound by oath or affirmation to support this Constitution; but no religious test shall ever be required as a qualification to any office or public trust under the United States.

ARTICLE VII

The ratification of the Conventions of nine States shall be sufficient for the establishment of this Constitution between the States so ratifying the same.

Done in Convention, by the unanimous consent of the States present, the seventeenth day of September, in the year of our Lord one thousand seven hundred and eighty-seven, and of the independence of the United States of America the twelfth.

AMENDMENTS

(The first ten amendments, known as the Bill of Rights, were proposed at the first session of the first Congress of the United States and were duly ratified by the required number of states by December, 1791.)

AMENDMENT I

Congress shall make no law respecting an establishment of religion, or prohibiting the free exercise thereof; or abridging the freedom of speech, or the press; or the right of the people peaceably to assemble, and to petition the government for redress of grievances.

AMENDMENT II

A well-regulated militia being necessary to the security of a free State, the right of the people to keep and bear arms shall not be infringed.

AMENDMENT III

No soldier shall, in time of peace, be quartered in any house, without the consent of the owner; nor in time of war but in a manner to be prescribed by law.

AMENDMENT IV

The right of the people to be secure in their persons, houses, papers, and effects, against unreasonable searches and seizures, shall not be violated, and no warrants shall issue, but upon probable cause, supported by oath or affirmation, and particularly describing the place to be searched, and the persons or things to be seized.

AMENDMENT V

No person shall be held to answer for a capital, or otherwise infamous crime, unless on a presentment or indictment of a grand jury, except in cases arising in the land or naval forces, or in the militia, when in actual service in time of war and public danger; nor shall any person be subject for the same offence to be twice put in jeopardy of life or limb; nor shall be compelled in any criminal case to be a witness against himself, nor to be deprived of life, liberty, or property, without due process of law; nor shall private property be taken for public use, without just compensation.

AMENDMENT VI

In all criminal prosecutions, the accused shall enjoy the right to a speedy and public trial, by an impartial jury of the State and district wherein the crime shall have been committed, which district shall have been previously ascertained by law, and to be informed of the nature and cause of the accusation; to be confronted with the witnesses against him; to have compulsory process for obtaining witnesses in his favor, and to have the assistance of counsel for his defence.

AMENDMENT VII

In suits at common law, where the value in controversy shall exceed twenty dollars, the right of trial by jury shall be preserved, and no fact tried by a jury shall be otherwise re-examined in any court of the United States than according to the rules of common law.

AMENDMENT VIII

Excessive bail shall not be required, nor excessive fines imposed, nor cruel and unusual punishments inflicted.

AMENDMENT IX

The enumeration in the Constitution of certain rights shall not be construed to deny or disparage others retained by the people.

AMENDMENT X

The powers not delegated to the United States by the Constitution, nor prohibited by it to the States, are reserved to the States respectively, or to the people.

AMENDMENT XI

The judicial power of the United States shall not be construed to extend to any suit in law or equity, commenced or prosecuted against one of the United States by citizens of another State, or by citizens or subjects of any foreign State. (Adopted in 1798)

AMENDMENT XII

The electors shall meet in their respective States, and vote by ballot for President and Vice-President, one of whom, at least, shall not be an inhabitant of the same State with themselves; they shall name in their ballots the person voted for as President, and in distinct ballots the persons voted for as Vice-President; and they shall make distinct lists of all persons voted for as President, and of all persons voted for as Vice-President, and of the number of votes for each, which list they shall sign and certify, and transmit sealed to the seat of the government of the United States, directed to the president of the Senate;—the president of the Senate shall, in the presence of the Senate and House of Representatives, open all the certificates, and the votes shall then be counted;—the person having the greatest number of votes for President shall be the

President, if such number be a majority of the whole number of electors appointed; and if no person have such majority, then from the persons having the highest numbers not exceeding three on the list of those voted for as President, the House of Representatives shall choose immediately, by ballot, the President. But in choosing the President, the votes shall be taken by States, the representation from each State having one vote; a quorum for this purpose shall consist of a member or members from two-thirds of the States, and a majority of all the States shall be necessary to a choice. And if the House of Representatives shall not choose a President whenever the right of choice shall devolve upon them, before the fourth day of March next following, then the Vice-President shall act as President, as in the case of the death or other constitutional disability of the President. The person having the greatest number of votes as Vice-President shall be the Vice-President, if such number be a majority of the whole number of electors appointed; and if no person have a majority, then from the two highest numbers on the list, the Senate shall choose the Vice-President; a quorum for the purpose shall consist of two-thirds of the whole number of senators, and a majority of the whole number shall be necessary to a choice. But no person constitutionally ineligible to the office of President shall be eligible to that of Vice-President of the United States. (Adopted in 1804)

AMENDMENT XIII

SECTION 1. Neither slavery nor involuntary servitude, except as a punishment for crime, whereof the party shall have been duly convicted, shall exist within the United States, or any place subject to their jurisdiction.

SECTION 2. Congress shall have power to enforce this article by appropriate legislation. (Adopted in 1865)

AMENDMENT XIV

SECTION 1. All persons born or naturalized in the United States, and subject to the jurisdiction thereof, are citizens of the United States and of the State wherein they reside. No State shall make or enforce any law which shall abridge the privileges or immunities of citizens of the United States; nor shall any State deprive any person of life, liberty, or property, without due process of law, nor deny to any person within its jurisdiction the equal protection of the laws.

SECTION 2. Representatives shall be appointed among the several States according to their respective numbers, counting the whole number of persons in each State, excluding Indians not taxed. But when the right to vote at any election for the choice of electors for President and Vice-President of the United States, representatives in Congress, the executive or judicial officers of a State, or the members of the Legislature thereof, is denied to any of the male inhabitants of such State, being twenty-one years of age, and citizens of the United States, or in any way abridged, except for participation in rebellion or other crime, the basis of representation therein shall be reduced in the proportion which the number of such male citizens shall bear to the whole number of male citizens twenty-one years of age in such State.

SECTION 3. No person shall be a senator or representative in Congress, or elector of President or Vice-President, or hold any office, civil or military, under the United States, or under any State, who having previously taken an oath as a member of Congress, or as an officer of the United States, or as a member of any State Legislature, or as an executive or judicial officer of any State, to support the Constitution of the United States, shall have engaged in insurrection or rebellion against the same, or given aid or comfort to the enemies thereof. But Congress may, by a vote of two-thirds of each house, remove such disability.

SECTION 4. The validity of the public debt of the United States, authorized by law, including debts incurred for payment of pensions and bounties for services in suppressing insurrection or rebellion, shall not be questioned. But neither the United States nor any State shall assume or pay any debt or obligation incurred in aid of insurrection or rebellion against the United States, or any claim for the loss or emancipation of any slave; but all such debts, obligations, and claims shall be held illegal and void.

SECTION 5. Congress shall have power to enforce, by appropriate legislation, the provisions of this article. (Adopted in 1868)

AMENDMENT XV

SECTION 1. The rights of citizens of the United States to vote shall not be denied or abridged by the United States, or by any State, on account of race, color, or previous condition of servitude.

SECTION 2. Congress shall have power to enforce this article by appropriate legislation. (Adopted in 1870)

AMENDMENT XVI

The Congress shall have power to lay and collect taxes on incomes, from whatever source derived, without apportionment among the several States, and without regard to any census or enumeration. (Adopted in 1913)

AMENDMENT XVII

SECTION 1. The Senate of the United States shall be composed of two senators from each State, elected by the people thereof, for six years; and each senator shall have one vote.

The electors in each State shall have the qualifications requisite for electors of the most numerous branch of the State Legislatures.

SECTION 2. When vacancies happen in the representation of any State in the Senate, the executive authority of such State shall issue writs of election to fill such vacancies: Provided, That the Legislature of any State may empower the executive thereof to make temporary appointment until the people fill the vacancies by election as the Legislature may direct.

SECTION 3. This amendment shall not be so construed as to affect the election or term of any senator chosen before it becomes valid as part of the Constitution. (Adopted in 1913)

AMENDMENT XVIII*

SECTION 1. After one year from the ratification of this article the manufacture, sale, or transportation of intoxicating liquors within, the importation thereof into, or the exportation thereof from the United States and all territory subject to the jurisdiction thereof for beverage purposes is hereby prohibited.

SECTION 2. The Congress and the several States shall have concurrent power to enforce this article by appropriate legislation.

SECTION 3. This article shall be inoperative unless it shall have been ratified as an amendment to the Constitution by the Legislatures of the several States, as provided by the Constitution, within seven years from the date of the submission hereof to the States by the Congress. (Adopted in 1919)

---

*This amendment has been superseded by Amendment XXI.

AMENDMENT XIX

SECTION 1. The rights of citizens of the United States to vote shall not be denied or abridged by the United States or by any State on account of sex.

SECTION 2. Congress shall have power, by appropriate legislation, to enforce the provisions of this article. (Adopted in 1920)

AMENDMENT XX

SECTION 1. The terms of the President and Vice-President shall end at noon on the twentieth day of January, and the terms of Senators and Representatives at noon on the third day of January of the years in which such terms would have ended if this article had not been ratified; and the terms of their successors shall then begin.

SECTION 2. The Congress shall assemble at least once in every year, and such meeting shall begin at noon on the third day of January, unless they shall by law appoint a different day.

SECTION 3. If, at the time fixed for the beginning of the term of the President, the President-elect shall have died, the Vice-President-elect shall become President. If a President shall not have been chosen before the time fixed for the beginning of his term, or if the President-elect shall have failed to qualify, then the Vice-President-elect shall act as President until a President shall have qualified; and the Congress may by law provide for the case wherein neither a President-elect nor a Vice-President-elect shall have qualified, declaring who shall then act as President, or the manner in which one who is to act shall be selected, and such person shall act accordingly until a President or Vice-President shall have qualified.

SECTION 4. The Congress may by law provide for the case of the death of any of the persons from whom the House of

Representatives may choose a President whenever the right of choice shall have devolved upon them, and for the case of the death of any of the persons from whom the Senate may choose a Vice-President whenever the right of choice shall have devolved upon them.

SECTION 5. Sections 1 and 2 shall take effect on the fifteenth day of October following the ratification of this article.

SECTION 6. This article shall be inoperative unless it shall have been ratified as an amendment to the Constitution by the Legislatures of three-fourths of the several States within seven years from the date of its submission. (Adopted in 1933)

AMENDMENT XXI

SECTION 1. The eighteenth article of amendment to the Constitution of the United States is hereby repealed.

SECTION 2. The transportation or importation into any State, Territory, or Possession of the United States for delivery or use therein of intoxicating liquors, in violation of the laws thereof, is hereby prohibited.

SECTION 3. This article shall be inoperative unless it shall have been ratified as an amendment to the Constitution by conventions in the several States, as provided in the Constitution, within seven years from the date of the submission hereof to the states by the Congress. (Adopted in 1933)

Quotations from WASHINGTON'S "FAREWELL ADDRESS"

The period for a new election of a citizen to administer the executive government of the United States being not far distant, and the time actually arrived when your thoughts must be employed in designating the person who is to be clothed with that important trust, it appears to me proper, especially as it may conduce to a more distinct expression of the public voice, that I should now apprise you of the resolution I have formed, to decline being considered among the number of those out of whom a choice is to be made. . . .

The acceptance of, and continuance hitherto in the office to which your suffrages have twice called me, have been a uniform sacrifice of inclination to the opinion of duty, and to a deference for what appeared to be your desire. I constantly hoped that it would have been much earlier in my power, consistently with motives which I was not at liberty to disregard, to return to that retirement from which I had been reluctantly drawn. The strength of my inclination to do this, previous to the last election, had even led to the preparation of an address to declare it to you; but mature reflection on the then perplexed and critical posture of our affairs with foreign nations, and the unanimous advice of persons entitled to my confidence, impelled me to abandon the idea.

I rejoice that the state of your concerns, external as well as internal, no longer renders the pursuit of inclination incompatible with the sentiment of duty or propriety; and am persuaded, whatever partiality may be retained for my services, that, in the present circumstances of our country, you will not disapprove my determination to retire. . . .

Here, perhaps, I ought to stop. But a solicitude for your welfare, which cannot end but with my life, and the apprehension of danger, natural to that solicitude, urge me, on an occasion like the present, to offer to your solemn contemplation, and to recommend to your frequent review, some sentiments, which are the result of much reflection, of no inconsiderable observation, and which appear to me all-important to the permanency of your felicity as a people. These will be offered to you with the more freedom, as you can only see in them the disinterested warnings of a parting friend, who can possibly have no personal motive to bias his counsel. . . .

Interwoven as is the love of liberty with every ligament of your hearts, no recommendation of mine is necessary to fortify or confirm the attachment.

The unity of government, which constitutes you one people, is also now dear to you. It is justly so; for it is a main pillar in the edifice of your real independence, the support of your tranquillity at home, your peace abroad; of your safety; of your prosperity; of that very liberty which you so highly prize. But as it is easy to foresee that, from different causes and from different quarters, much pains will be taken, many artifices employed, to weaken in your minds the conviction of this truth; as this is the point in your political fortress against which the batteries of internal and external enemies will be most constantly and actively (though often covertly and insidiously) directed, it is of infinite moment that you should properly estimate the immense value of your national union to your collective and individual happiness; that you should cherish a cordial, habitual, and immovable attachment to it; accustoming yourselves to think and speak of it as of the palladium of your political safety and prosperity; watching for its preservation with jealous anxiety; discountenancing whatever may suggest even a suspicion that it can in any event be abandoned; and indignantly frowning upon the first dawning of every attempt to alienate any portion of our country from the rest, or to enfeeble the sacred ties which now link together the various parts. . . .

While, then, every part of our country thus feels an immediate and particular interest in union, all the parts combined cannot fail to find in the united mass of means and efforts greater strength, greater resource, proportionably greater security from external danger, a less frequent interruption of their peace by foreign nations, and, what is of inestimable value, they must derive from union an exemption from those broils and wars between themselves, which so frequently afflict neighboring countries not tied together by the same governments, which their own rivalships alone would be sufficient to produce, but which opposite foreign alliances, attachments, and intrigues would stimulate and embitter. Hence, likewise, they will avoid the necessity of those overgrown military establishments which, under any form of government, are inauspicious to liberty, and which are to be regarded as particularly hostile to republican liberty. In this sense it is, that your union ought to be considered as a main prop of your liberty, and that the love of the one ought to endear to you the preservation of the other. . . .

In contemplating the causes which may disturb our Union, it occurs as a matter of serious concern, that any ground should have been furnished for characterizing parties by geographical discriminations, Northern and Southern, Atlantic and Western; whence designing men may endeavor to excite a belief that there is a real difference of local interests and views. . . .

To the efficacy and permanency of your union, a government for the whole is indispensable. No alliances, however strict, between the parts can be an adequate substitute. Sensible of this momentous truth, you have improved upon your first essay, by the adoption of a constitution of government better calculated than your former for an intimate union, and for the efficacious management of your common concerns. This government, the offspring of our own choice, uninfluenced and unawed, adopted upon full investigation and mature deliberation, completely free in its principles, in the distribution of its powers, uniting security with energy, and containing within itself a provision for its own amendment, has a just claim to your confidence and your support. Respect for its authority, compliance with its laws, acquiescence in its measures, are duties enjoined by the fundamental maxims of true Liberty. The basis of our political systems is the right of the people to make and to alter their constitutions of government. But the constitution which at any time exists, till changed by an explicit and authentic act of the whole people, is sacredly obligatory upon all. The very idea of the power and the right of the people to establish government presupposes the duty of every individual to obey the established government. . . .

Towards the preservation of your government, and the permanency of your present happy state, it is requisite, not only that you steadily discountenance irregular opposition to its acknowledged authority, but also that you resist with care the spirit of innovation upon its principles, however specious the pretexts. One method of assault may be to effect, in the forms of the Constitution, alterations which will impair the energy of the system, and thus to undermine what cannot be directly overthrown. . . .

I have already intimated to you the danger of parties in the State, with particular reference to the founding of them on geographical discriminations. Let me now take a more comprehensive view, and warn you in the most solemn manner against the baneful effects of the spirit of party, generally.

This spirit, unfortunately, is inseparable from our nature, having its root in the strongest passions of the human mind. It exists under different shapes in all governments, more or less stifled, controlled, or repressed; but in those of the popular form it is seen in its greatest rankness, and is truly their worst enemy.

The alternate domination of one faction over another,

sharpened by the spirit of revenge natural to party dissension, which in different ages and countries has perpetrated the most horrid enormities, is itself a frightful despotism. But this leads at length to a more formal and permanent despotism. The disorders and miseries which result gradually incline the minds of men to seek security and repose in the absolute power of an individual; and sooner or later the chief of some prevailing faction, more able or more fortunate than his competitors, turns this disposition to the purposes of his own elevation on the ruins of public liberty.

Without looking forward to an extremity of this kind (which nevertheless ought not to be entirely out of sight), the common and continual mischiefs of the spirit of party are sufficient to make it the interest and duty of a wise people to discourage and restrain it. . . .

There is an opinion that parties in free countries are useful checks upon the administration of the government and serve to keep alive the spirit of liberty. This within certain limits is probably true, and, in governments of a monarchical cast, patriotism may look with indulgence, if not with favor, upon the spirit of party. But in those of the popular character, in governments purely elective, it is a spirit not to be encouraged. From their natural tendency, it is certain there will always be enough of that spirit for every salutary purpose. And, there being constant danger of excess, the effort ought to be, by force of public opinion, to mitigate and assuage it. A fire not to be quenched, it demands a uniform vigilance to prevent its bursting into a flame, lest, instead of warming, it should consume.

It is important, likewise, that the habits of thinking in a free country should inspire caution in those entrusted in its administration, to confine themselves within their respective constitutional spheres, avoiding in the exercise of the powers of one department to encroach upon another. The spirit of encroachment tends to consolidate the powers of all the departments in one, and thus to create, whatever the form of government, a real despotism. A just estimate of that love of power, and proneness to abuse it, which predominates in the human heart, is sufficient to satisfy us of the truth of this position. The necessity of reciprocal checks in the exercise of political power, by dividing and distributing it into different depositories, and constituting each the guardian of the public weal against invasions by the others, has been evinced by experiments ancient and modern, some of them in our country and under our own eyes. To preserve them must be as necessary as to institute them. If, in the opinion of the people, the distribution or modification of the constitutional powers be in any particular wrong, let it be corrected by an amendment in the way which the Constitution designates. But let there be no change by usurpation; for, though this, in one instance, may be the instrument of good, it is the customary weapon by which free governments are destroyed. The precedent must always greatly overbalance in permanent evil any partial or transient benefit which the use can at any time yield. . . .

Promote, then, as an object of primary importance, institutions for the general diffusion of knowledge. In proportion as the structure of a government gives force to public opinion, it is essential that public opinion should be enlightened.

As a very important source of strength and security, cherish public credit. One method of preserving it is to use it as sparingly as possible; avoiding occasions of expense by cultivating peace, but remembering also that timely disbursements to prepare for danger frequently prevent much greater disbursements to repel it; avoiding likewise the accumulation of debt, not only by shunning occasions of expense, but by vigorous exertions in time of peace to discharge the debts which unavoidable wars may have occasioned, not ungenerously throwing upon posterity the burden which we ourselves ought to bear. The execution of these maxims belongs to your representatives, but it is necessary that public opinion should co-operate. To facilitate to them the performance of their duty, it is essential that you should practically bear in mind that towards the payment of debts there must be revenue; that to have revenue there must be taxes; that no taxes can be devised which are not more or less inconvenient and unpleasant. . . .

Observe good faith and justice towards all nations; cultivate peace and harmony with all. Religion and morality enjoin this conduct; and can it be that good policy does not equally enjoin it? It will be worthy of a free, enlightened, and, at no distant period, a great nation, to give to mankind the magnanimous and too novel example of a people always guided by an exalted justice and benevolence. . . .

In the execution of such a plan, nothing is more essential than that permanent, inveterate antipathies against particular nations, and passionate attachments for others, should be excluded; and that, in place of them, just and amicable feelings towards all should be cultivated. . . .

Against the insidious wiles of foreign influence (I conjure you to believe me, fellow-citizens), the jealousy of a free people ought to be constantly awake, since history and experience prove that foreign influence is one of the most baneful foes of republican government. But that jealousy, to be useful, must be impartial; else it becomes the instrument of the very influence to be avoided, instead of a defense against it. Excessive partiality for one foreign nation, and excessive dislike of another, cause those whom they actuate to see danger only on one side, and serve to veil and even second the arts of influence on the other. Real patriots who may resist the intrigues of the favorite are liable to become suspected and odious; while its tools and dupes usurp the applause and confidence of the people, to surrender their interests.

The great rule of conduct for us, in regard to foreign nations, is, in extending our commercial relations, to have with them as little political connections as possible. So far as we have already formed engagements, let them be fulfilled with perfect good faith. Here let us stop. . . .

It is our true policy to steer clear of permanent alliances with any portion of the foreign world; so far, I mean, as we are now at liberty to do it; for let me not be understood as capable of patronizing infidelity to existing engagements. I hold the maxim no less applicable to public than to private affairs, that honesty is always the best policy. I repeat it, therefore, let those engagements be observed in their genuine sense. But, in my opinion, it is unnecessary and would be unwise to extend them.

Taking care always to keep ourselves, by suitable establishments, in a respectable defensive posture, we may safely trust to temporary alliances for extraordinary emergencies.

Harmony, liberal intercourse with all nations, are recommended by policy, humanity, and interest. But even our commercial policy should hold an equal and impartial hand, neither seeking nor granting exclusive favors or preferences. . . . There can be no greater error than to expect or calculate upon real favors from nation to nation.   It is an illusion which experience must cure, which a just pride ought to discard.

In offering to you, my countrymen, these counsels of an old and affectionate friend, I dare not hope they will make the strong and lasting impression I could wish; that they will control the usual current of the passions, or prevent our nation from running the course which has hitherto marked the destiny of nations. But, if I may even flatter myself that they may be productive of some partial benefit, some occasional good; that they may now and then recur to moderate the fury of party spirit, to warn against the mischiefs of foreign intrigue, to guard against the impostures of pretended patriotism; this hope will be a full recompense for the solicitude for your welfare, by which they have been dictated. . . .